REDBACK QUARTERLY 9

GENERATION LESS

HOW AUSTRALIA IS CHEATING THE YOUNG

Jennifer Rayner

Published by Redback Quarterly,
an imprint of Schwartz Publishing Pty Ltd
Level 1, 221 Drummond Street
Carlton VIC 3053, Australia
enquiries@blackincbooks.com
www.redbackquarterly.com.au

National Library of Australia Cataloguing-in-Publication entry:
Rayner, Jennifer, author.
Generation less: how Australia is cheating the young/Jennifer Rayner.
9781863958127 (paperback)
9781925203868 (ebook)
Subjects: Youth–Australia.
Youth–Government policy–Australia.
Australia–Economic policy.

305.2350994

Cover design by Peter Long
Cover image from Dreamstime
Text design and typesetting by Tristan Main

For Patrick – and all the young Australians like him.
And for Luka, that he might know a fairer future.

CONTENTS

INTRODUCTION

I will be 30 soon. At that age my mum and dad were settled, prosperous parents of three. Home-owners; tenured workers tucking away super and long service leave; possessors of both everyday and special-occasion cutlery.

I see now that they were the benchmark I instinctively set my expectations against. Growing up in the striving suburbia of Hawke and Howard, I never doubted that my friends and I would lead lives that eclipsed theirs. I didn't doubt we'd continue the golden trend tracing back to the Great Depression, yet another Australian generation to enjoy more wealth and opportunity than our parents did.

I doubt it now.

As I look around the bar on a Friday after five, I see none of the steady satisfaction that brimmed from my parents and their peers. Instead, I see young people squeezed by creeping pressures not of their making and largely beyond their control. I find 20-somethings living out an ever-extending adolescence as the building blocks for a stable, comfortable life slip further from their reach. I hear brittle laughter at black jokes about renting till 50 and retiring beyond the grave.

I see my generation becoming the first in over 80 years to go backwards in work, wealth and wellbeing.

This book is not a whine from entitled Generation Y. If you're already firing up to dismiss it in those terms, stay your snark for a moment. This book is a warning about the waves of demographic, economic and social change that are already breaking over young Australians. Left unchecked, these changes will lead to rising intergenerational inequality in this country. Just as we have seen a growing gap between rich and poor over recent decades, we're beginning to see young and old pull apart in ways that will wear at our communal bonds.

If you're uncomfortable taking a young woman's word for it, allow me to deliver you the same message from an old white man instead. In February 2014, leading economist and Deloitte Access Economics director Chris Richardson told the *Australian Financial Review*: 'There is a stunning generational unfairness in our settings, and all those disengaged young Australians need to wake up to the fact they're being massively screwed.'[1]

It isn't just young Australians who need to wake up to this fact. It's all of us. This country is so busy planning for the looming grey tsunami that we're letting an entire generation fall behind. If we don't think harder about building a future for the old *and* the young, my friends and I will be just the first of many generations to face lives of shrinking opportunity.

I don't believe Australians want that. I think we want to be a country that does right by all its people; a community that can take care of the old without making second-class citizens of the young. To do that, we first need to recognise where we're going wrong. Then we need to find the will to fix it.

In this book I'll try to kindle that will by demonstrating just how much this country's current trends and settings skew against the young. In later sections, I'll also offer ideas for bringing about a better intergenerational balance. Coming as they do from someone who works for the Australian Labor Party, these ideas are informed by the values of fairness, egalitarianism and opportunity that that political movement embodies. But they are not party proposals only partisans could love. Some are ideas that governments of very different political lineages have tried elsewhere in the world. Others come not from the world of politics at all, but rather from fields like tech and town planning. Each could lessen at least some of the pressure bearing down on young Australians, to ensure we remain a country where young men and women can flourish.

At its most fundamental, that is what intergenerational equality means: young Australians having the same opportunities to build stable, secure lives as our parents and grandparents enjoyed before us. The unequal alternative will see young people become bystanders to Australia's prosperity as older people claim more and more of its building blocks.

THE GREAT GREYING OF AUSTRALIA

One reason inequality between the generations is such a risk today is hard demographics: people in their autumn years will soon outnumber those in their salad days. You'd have to be a hermit on a hillside not to have noticed that Australia's population is ageing, but the 2015 Intergenerational Report showed just how much this is going to change the face of our community in the next forty years. By 2055 the number of Australians aged over 65 is set to double, as sprightly pensioners live on into their 80s, 90s and beyond. Today, there are 4.5 Australians of working age for every oldie over 65. Four decades from now that number will have almost halved, to just 2.7 working tax-payers for every retiree. People over 60 will well outnumber those under 20 by the time a baby born today grapples with their mid-life crisis.[2]

All this getting older will be pricey. The federal government will need to cover new spending equivalent to 4.4 per cent of GDP to fund all the hip replacements and mushy apples this burgeoning cohort of ancients will need.[3] State governments will need to stump up further spending equivalent to 1.4 per cent of GDP. It is this challenge that led former Treasurer Joe Hockey to ponder in a TV interview: 'How can we afford the future? How are our children going to be able to afford the future?'[4]

It is undeniably important for us to plan for an ageing Australia. But what's lacking from the current discussion is any real concern for how young people will be affected today and tomorrow by policies designed with the old in mind. What's more, in the panic about Australia's rising grey tide we seem to be overlooking trends in our economy and society that are already making life harder for the young. As I'll show, a major redistribution of resources and opportunity is underway from my generation to those of my parents and grandparents. Allowing that to continue unchecked can only be harmful for our collective future.

A NOTE ABOUT GENERATIONS

In laying out the evidence for the growing gap between young and old, I'll talk a lot about my 'generation' and those that came before it. I use that term carefully, according to its original meaning: to describe the turn of years from parent to child. This 'small-g' definition captures the idea of human progression: parents and their children, the young growing up to beget young of their own, down the decades that make up our communal story.

This shouldn't be confused with the 'big-G' generationalism of the Baby Boomers, X-ers, Millennials and more. This book tries to stay away from the ordnance-strewn trenches of those generation wars; talking about big-G generations can muddy things more often than it adds meaning.[5]

To understand what's going wrong in Australia, we need to distinguish between 'life cycle' and 'cohort' effects. An age cohort is a group of people born at a particular time – in the same year, decade or era of change. The people in that group share some characteristics because they are partially shaped by the common experiences of their lives. Like many children of the early '90s, I'll never be able to unlearn the words to the theme from *The Fresh Prince of Bel-Air*, or forget the unique disappointment of seeing a Hypercolor T-shirt lose its lustre in the wash.

The important point is that cohort effects persist over time – a Fresh Prince fan at age nine maintains an abiding affection for Will Smith at 29. That links me to other childhood fans and sets us all apart in some small way from an older friend of mine, who spent her after-school hours watching *M*A*S*H* (developing a lifelong fetish for lanky men with sandy moustaches in the process).

On the other hand, as the mother of an under-five, I also have plenty in common with every harried parent who has ever tried to cram toast into a toddler's mouth while hopping out the door with just one shoe on. Experiencing the daily trials and victories of this particular stage of life, I find common ground with people born decades before me and those who are still to come. That commonality is the definition of a life cycle effect.

With life cycle effects, the traits we share with others change as we bowl through the years. Right now, I care as passionately about childcare as any parent who leaves their tiny beloved in the hands of strangers for eight hours a day. But by the time I'm 55, I expect to be just as bored by talk of care ratios and early learning outcomes as my parents are today.

What's true of attitudes and tastes is true of tangible things too. For example, young people almost always have less wealth than their parents because they've had fewer years to acquire it. Being pov in your 20s is a life cycle effect. As economist John Quiggin notes:

> Most of the time, [life cycle] effects are more important than cohort effects. The primary schoolers of the 1960s were very like the primary schoolers of today and, of course, totally different from the middle-aged parents they have become. The grandparents of today are more like their own grandparents than the bodgies and widgies they may have been in the 1950s.[6]

On one level, Quiggin is right. Noughties schoolkids are just as obsessed with inventing arcane bullying rituals as schoolkids 50 years ago were; nanas of the 1960s loved nosing into other people's lives as much as mine does today. However, it is often assumed that these life cycle common-alities always hold true across our finances, work and wellbeing too. It is all but expected that each new cohort of Australians will make the same successful progression from striving youth to comfortable retirement as those who've come before us.

That can only happen if young people today have comparable *opportunities* to the young in decades past. To get to where our parents and grandparents have by the same age, my generation and those coming after us would need to have been dealt a roughly equal hand.

But as I'll argue throughout this book, economic, demographic and technological trends mean the deck is actually heavily stacked against us. Worse, the dud cards are mounting up all the time. In the coming pages I'll show how life cycle effects in work, wealth and wellbeing are growing more significant, dramatically increasing disparities between the young and the old. I'll also show how the huge escalation in the price of housing and education is placing an enduring handicap on the cohorts born from the 1980s onwards. As a result, we are likely to fare worse than the cohorts of our parents and grandparents at 35, 55 and beyond.

Things have changed in this country. Australia is no longer the nation of easy opportunity that those before us came up in. The growing gaps between young and old are fundamentally reshaping the lives of we who are young today. If we can get those gaps closing again, my cohort will be just a blip in Australia's demographic history, a rare backwards step in our long march of progress. But if we don't, those coming after us will know less opportunity still, relegated to live in the shadow of prosperity instead of sharing it. Generation after generation will do worse than the last if we don't tackle the inequality gaps now.

*

When I first pitched the idea of this book to an economist mentor of mine, his face assumed that affectionately patronising look you give a kid who can't find the toy that's sitting on the table in front of them. 'But these are just trends,' he said. 'A black swan event could change the trajectory of any of them.' In Nassim Nicholas Taleb's telling, a black swan event is something rare and unexpected that diverts the course of everything that comes after it.[7] Taleb cites the rise of the internet and the September 11 terrorist attacks as two events we simply didn't see coming. As a society, all we could do was adapt in their wake once they had changed the world as we knew it. Flapping around the idea of black swan events was my mate's way of saying that today's trends are no firm guide to what will happen tomorrow.

He's right – we don't know the future. Another major financial crisis may wipe out the growing wealth gap between older and younger Australians. A shift in technology might suddenly render people over 40 unemployable. A hegira of exiles from catastrophe elsewhere could switch our demographic mix overnight.

But does that absolve us from taking steps to counter the worrying trends we see today? Of course it doesn't. Rising inequality between the old and the young is a real risk, and one that will fray our social fabric. Ignoring the problems I'll raise in these pages in the hope they'll somehow fix themselves is the laziest kind of wishful thinking.

So pay attention. Please. A country that makes no room for the young is a country that will forfeit a fair future. This must not become Australia.

CHAPTER ONE
WORK (GETTING IN)

Some things I gained in five years juggling multiple jobs in restaurants and bars: a revulsion for the milky-sweet smell of Baileys. The ability to count up to 20 in Thai. A sixth sense about which ones will be waiting for you in the car park at the end of your shift. Things I did not gain: more than $3000 in superannuation. Sick leave. Permanent work or transferable skills.

My time as a casual worker in strip-lit kitchens and gummy-floored bars was mercifully brief compared with that of some of my friends, who are still pulling beers as our 30s loom. It paid the bills (just) while I studied, gave me somewhere to go between lectures and gin binges and kept me from relying too heavily on the grudging beneficence of Centrelink. In truth, I remember only bits and pieces about the individual jobs. I was always tired and often hung-over, forever on the verge of tears or mania from the sheer bloody effort of keeping my newly adult self together. But what clings to those years like a sour incense is the memory of how utterly powerless I felt.

I could do nothing when the manager called at 8 a.m. to say I wouldn't be needed that day. I had no recourse when I was sent to work in the smoking lounge of the pub despite asthma that had me gasping for air by the end of my shift. I had little option but to agree when the boss suggested I'd be better off getting paid cash in hand with no tax questions asked. Throughout those years, if I was sick: that was my problem. If I couldn't make a shift: there were often no more after that. If I had a concern, a complaint or even a question: no one wanted to hear it.

That powerlessness is what hundreds of thousands of young Australians feel as they try to navigate their first steps into the job market. Economics editor of the *Australian* David Uren argues it is now harder for young people to get reliable, well-paid work than at any time in the past 20 years – and back then there was a vast recession on.[1] Many of the doorways that our parents and grandparents passed through on their way to full employment have been closed and bricked up for good.

That's because the world of work is changing; everyone knows this. We feel it like an absence, a growing blank space at the centre of our economic life. Those old enough to remember the offices and factory floors of the '80s sense it in the quiet that fell after the ticking of typewriters and the grinding of big machinery ceased. The awareness seeps into those of us who've joined the job market more recently through the growing drought of permanent positions, the ceaseless hustle for that next contract role, the pressure to update skills we've only just attained. That change is a fact, like gravity or the earworm quality of ABBA songs. As I'll discuss later, it is the product of structural and technological tides that no country can entirely levee against.

But while the changing nature of work affects us all, not all of us have been equally affected. Rather, Australians in their late teens and 20s have lost far more ground than others. In this chapter, I'll show that the gap between green workers and grey ones is widening on measures of underemployment, wage growth and casualisation. Taken together, these trends risk creating a working underclass of the young.

HARDLY WORKING

Young people have always had it hardest in the job market, a consequence of having fewer skills, less experience and limited contacts. That's one reason why, since the late 1970s, the unemployment rate has averaged just 4.3 per cent for people between 45 and 54 but 10.2 per cent for Australians in their early 20s.[2] Young people's engagement in the workforce is also complicated by the fact that many spend their days in either full- or part-time study, just as I did. This means the need for work among people in their 20s varies far more than for older Australians.

In the past few years, the jobs debate in Australia has been dominated by the headline youth unemployment figure. Since the peak of the global financial crisis, our youth unemployment rate has been stubbornly high at an average of 11.2 per cent.[3] In blighted places like Burnie and Cairns, youth unemployment has hovered around 20 per cent, effectively keeping whole year groups and footy teams out of the job market.

At a time when the total unemployment rate averaged just 5.3 per cent, public handwringing about these figures is understandable. But as plenty of economists have pointed out, the unemployment rate doesn't always paint the most accurate picture of what's really going on with young people and work.[4] That's because it is calculated as a percentage of the *labour force* instead of the *total number of people* in their teens and early 20s. The labour force figure only takes in those who are working or looking for a job. People who are studying or spending a gap year making bad decisions on the beaches of Thailand aren't included in the count.

That's not to say that youth unemployment isn't a problem in Australia. You'd have to be a truly hardened Ayn Rand acolyte to be comfortable with the idea that around 300,000 young people were looking for a job in 2015 and couldn't find one. It's simply to point out that unemployment figures aren't the best or only guide to what's happening with young people and work in Australia today.

To better understand why 20-somethings are finding it increasingly hard-going in the workforce, we need to look to the figures on underemployment and casualisation. These show a growing gulf between young and older workers. What's more, the forces that are widening this gap seem only to be accelerating.

Underemployment is a handy yardstick with which to measure the health of the job market because it gauges how many people would work more hours if they could. Like in a lot of countries, Australia's data-gatherers consider you employed if you've worked at least one hour for pay in the past week. Of course, an hour's work is unlikely to cover a week's grocery bills (unless you're a corporate bigwig like the heads of the Commonwealth and ANZ banks, who each net more than $1200 an hour). So it's easily possible to have a job and still find yourself living in Penury Place.

Being underemployed might be preferable to having no work at all, but plenty of people will tell you that it's a stressful and grinding life. Underemployment is particularly rife in sectors like hospitality and retail, where shifts can get cut with a few minutes' notice if the customers aren't flowing. I once worked a waitressing job where my weekly hours ranged from 10 to 25 depending on how badly the business was going that week. On those paydays when my envelope had only a couple of yellow notes in it, I'd stuff stock cubes and dried shrimps from the restaurant's kitchen into my pockets on the way out the door. You can make a surprisingly tasty soup by boiling those ingredients with a kettle of Maggi noodles.

As with unemployment, there have always been more young Australians struggling to get enough work than older ones. In 1978, 3.2 per cent of people under 24 reported being underemployed, compared with 2 per cent of more seasoned workers aged between 45 and 54. Since then, underemployment has trended up for both age groups, but it has risen much further and faster for young people, reaching over 16 per cent in 2014. Where fewer than one in 30 young people said they were underemployed in the 1970s, the figure now stands at about one in six.[5]

As the chart below shows, in the late 1970s there was only a two-point gap in the percentage of young and older workers without enough work. The gap hovered around that level throughout the 1980s, but Keating's 'recession we had to have' saw it spike up to five points. Since then it has only continued to grow, reaching almost 10 points in 2014.

FIGURE 1: UNDEREMPLOYMENT IN AUSTRALIA

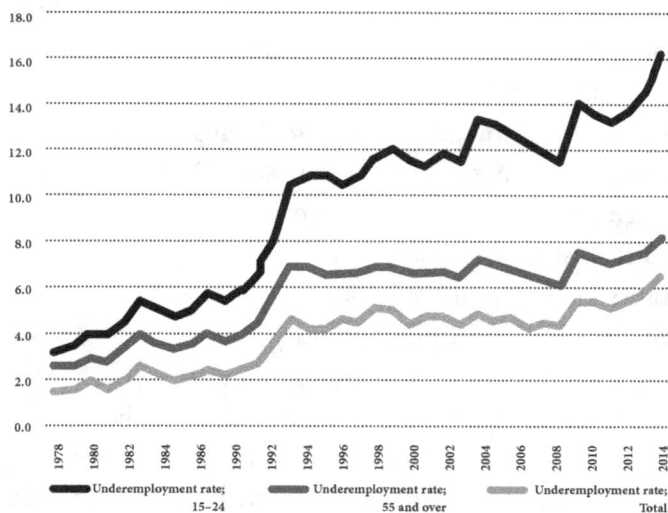

Underemployment rate; 15–24 · Underemployment rate; 55 and over · Underemployment rate; Total

Data: Australian Bureau of Statistics, Labour Force, Australia, cat: 6202.0

The most obvious and direct impact of underemployment is money; or rather, the lack of it. Having insufficient work means living payday to payday, with little or nothing left over at the end of each week to put aside. This leads to a reliance on credit cards to cover costs like uni books and bills, and loans when a car breaks down or a bond must be paid. As I show in Chapter 4, young Australians are carrying more debt than ever before. The escalating problem of underemployment is one reason so many of my peers can't get ahead financially.

The lack of money is one thing. But if you've ever had to mentally add up the cost of items in your trolley to make sure the meagre cash in your wallet will cover them, you'll know it's not just about shrunken purchasing power. The dread of going shopping, the anxiety about running out of petrol before payday, the uneasy wait for next week's roster – all of these things eat at your mental health as well. Backing this up, US researchers have found higher levels of stress and anxiety, along with more instances of depression, among people who don't have enough work.[6] If you find that surprising, try imagining a week where your maxed-out Amex couldn't cover Friday's post-work bottle of pinot. Major downer, right? Now substitute 'Amex' with 'amount left over after buying food', and 'pinot' with 'keeping the lights on'. Cue depression.

YOUNG CASUAL(TIE)S

Underemployment goes hand in hand with casual work. Permanent, salaried staff are paid a fixed wage, so bosses want to get their money's worth by having them work maximum hours. But because casual staff are paid by the hour, cutting their shifts is a quick way to save cash if trade isn't roaring. There has been an explosion of casual work in Australia over the past 25 years. Unfortunately, this has been almost entirely concentrated in the under-24 workforce.[7]

There are a number of different ways to define casual work. The Australian Bureau of Statistics bases it on whether a worker gets entitlements like holiday and sick pay on top of their salary. Working without these benefits is a strong sign that the job is casual. Someone is also counted as a casual if their hours can be varied week to week, and if they can be sacked without notice or access to redundancy entitlements. By that measure, the number of young people working casually in Australia has jumped from 34 per cent in 1992 to 50 per cent in 2013. Over the same period, the percentage of people working without entitlements in their later years has barely moved.[8] This has seen the casual work gap between young people and older Australians widen from 24 points when Paul Keating was PM to 37 points when Tony Abbott took over.

Figure 2: Workers without entitlements by age

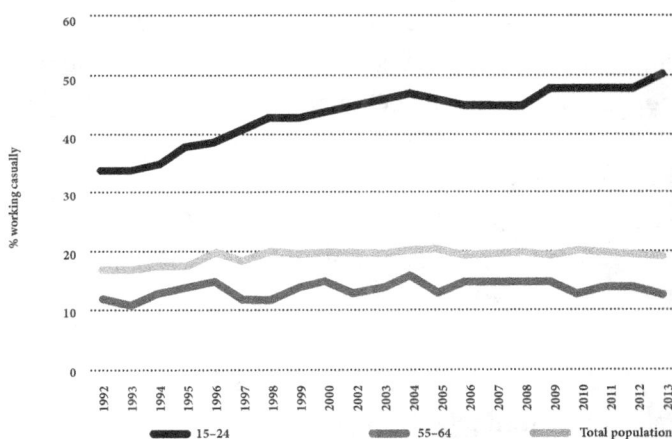

Data: Australian Bureau of Statistics, Australian Labour Market Statistics,
cat: 6105.0

Labour economists sometimes dismiss the rising casualisation of work as a by-product of more young Australians
going to university. Since more people in their late teens
and early 20s are studying, the argument goes, more of
them are looking for work that fits around classes and
keg-stands. There's no doubt that some of the rise in casual work has indeed been driven by people heading from
school into tertiary study, rather than straight into full-
time jobs. But this argument reduces the entire concept of
casual work to a question of hours and flexibility, when
there's actually more to it than that.

A few years ago the Australian Council of Trade Unions
held an inquiry into casual and insecure work. It found

that over half of all people working without entitlements were 'permanent casuals': people who worked at one place for long periods and had regular shifts, but missed out on any benefits by being badged as casual.[9] Many of these workers could have been classified as full- or part-time workers if their bosses had chosen to do so. Of course, this would have given the workers more rights and possibly cost their employers more money in the long run, so few businesses were rushing to do this.

In the same way, a university student working week-night and weekend shifts can easily be hired as a part-timer. It simply requires putting the rights and entitlements of workers on an equal footing with flexibility for business. Over the past 30 years, that balance has tipped decisively away from workers as total flexibility has become the *ne plus ultra* of industrial relations reform. *This* is the big shift that has pushed more young people into casual jobs than ever before. The jump in the number of young Australians going to university provides bosses with a convenient cover for working conditions that leave their employees much worse off.

The gaps that have opened up between young and old on measures of underemployment and casual work are worrying, but for the starkest illustration of the growing inequality, we simply need look at wages.

UNDERWORKED, UNDERPAID

Thanks to Thomas Piketty and those Occupy prats, you're probably aware that there's been a steady swelling in wage inequality across developed countries over the past few decades. In Australia, federal MP and former economics professor Andrew Leigh points out that between 1975 and 2014 real annual wages grew by $7000 for people in the bottom tenth of incomes, but by $47,000 for the top 10 per cent of earners. That means wages have only increased by 23 per cent for the lowest-paid Australians, while spiking 72 per cent for the highest-paid. As Leigh writes: 'If cleaners and checkout workers had received the same proportionate pay rise as solicitors and surgeons, they would be $16,000 a year better off.'[10]

While there's been plenty of fiery debate about this growing gap between the rich and the rest, I've yet to see anyone point out that wage inequality is also mushrooming between different age groups.

The gap is opening up because over the past two decades wage growth has been much slower for young workers than for their elders. Adjusted to 2013 dollars, weekly mean full-time earnings for people in their early 20s grew by $190 between 1990 and 2013. But for people in their early 50s, wages grew by $577.[11] In other words, weekly earnings for under-25s grew by just 25 per cent over the past 25 years, while increasing 59 per cent for people in their early 50s. There may be a pleasant symmetry to those numbers, but the disparity they've created between young and old is anything but pleasing.

For part-timers, the story is the same: weekly wages grew by $46 for people under 25 but by $205 for those over 50. That's wage growth of just 14 per cent for young workers against 40 per cent growth for older ones.[12]

FIGURE 3: WEEKLY EARNINGS BY AGE

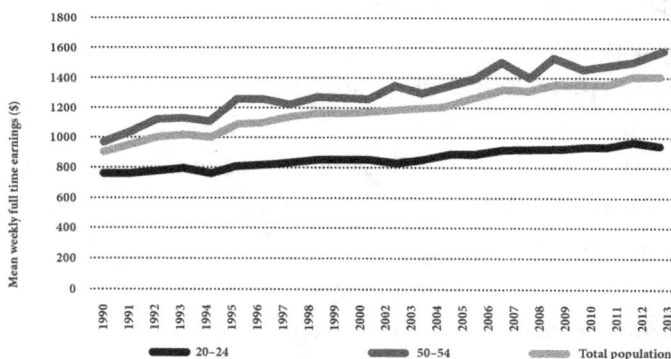

Data: Australian Bureau of Statistics, Employee Earnings, Benefits and Trade Union Membership, Australia, cat: 63100TS0002

I'll get to what's causing this wage gap in a moment, but it's worth lingering a while on what it means in hard dollars. In 1990, a 20-something worker who was fortunate enough to have got into the job market before the recession hit earned just over $750 a week in today's money. That's hardly high-rolling, but when you factor in that a worker pushing 55 was only earning about $220 a week more, it seems fair enough.

Skip ahead to 2013, and a full-time worker in their early 20s is earning $943 a week. Their grey-haired confrères have left them in their dust; average weekly wages in that age group have climbed to $1557. Older Australians now pocket more than $600 a week more than young workers – a fact that explains the emergence of all those god-awful '60s revival musicals, if nothing else.

If we're concerned about wage inequality across society as a whole, then we should also be worried about the growing gap between those at the start of their careers and those in late middle age. It's simply not fair that young people's wages should inch upwards while older people's rocket – particularly when the price of things like housing is also soaring higher than a speed freak at Splendour.

As I'll describe in coming chapters, insecure, insufficient work and poor wages are part of what's putting us on the back foot when it comes to buying a home, starting a business or paying back education debts. As the ability to start acquiring wealth recedes from us in our 20s, we're falling further behind our parents and grandparents, who had the wherewithal to set themselves up early.

NOT ON PURPOSE AIN'T NO EXCUSE

None of this is intentional. No dastardly government set out to design the difficult job market young Australians are struggling to enter today (although some have been blithely indifferent to how their policies have exacerbated the problem). It's just sour luck that there have been enormous structural changes in employment over the past 30 years; changes that have primarily hit the lower end of the job market, where young people seek a first foothold.

Inequality experts point to three causes of the blossoming gap between rich and poor: technology, globalisation and the decline of unions.[13] Those same three forces explain a good deal about the growing gaps between young and old in the Australian workforce.

Over the past few decades, technology and globalisation have combined to wipe out many of the blue- and white-collar jobs that once gave young people a leg-up into employment. Back when my parents finished school in the mid-1970s, people with fairly limited skills could expect to find steady work and get paid a decent wage for it. Whether assembling cars in Altona, canning fruit in Shepparton or answering phones in Canberra, there were secure, full-time jobs out there that didn't demand a lot of experience or higher learning.

Mechanisation and automation have now swallowed up a good chunk of those. Improvements in technology mean that factories can churn out many more cars and pluck plenty more chickens per hour than the factories of 30 years ago. But they need far fewer workers to do it. While manufacturing technology has been improving, Australia's governments have also been progressively dismantling the tariff walls that long served to keep out competing imports to Australian products. Now, I dig Spanish fast fashion and Korean electronics as much as the next impulse shopper. But there's no doubt our love of cheap overseas consumer goods has made it increasingly unprofitable to assemble, stitch or build them in Australia.

These twin trends – technology and globalisation – have slashed the number of low-skill, blue-collar jobs around today. In 1986, just under 1.1 million Australians worked in manufacturing; that's a bit over one in six out of all jobs at the time. The number has steadily trended down since then, even as our population has grown. By 2012 only 924,000 people still worked on a production line – around one in 12 Australian jobs.[14]

A host of entry-level white-collar jobs have been similarly abolished by better technology and a more borderless world. It'd be a rare and retrograde office that still had a typing pool of early-20s secretaries; most corporate call centres have now shifted offshore. Even higher-end work in professions like law and journalism is being disrupted as companies outsource document discovery and basic reporting to offshore freelancers, or dispense with humans outright in favour of machine-learned algorithms.[15]

With fewer of these starter jobs around, young people must instead go where there is still work available for those with limited skills. That means an increasing number clustering in hospitality, retail and the cheap end of the services sector – think nannying and nail bars. These positions are inherently less secure than the factory and office jobs of old, because they depend on seasonal and cyclical demand for dining out or spending up. To give just one example of this, the Australian retail sector shed roughly 50,000 jobs between February 2008 and May 2010 as the global financial crisis put a brake on consumer spending. Other sectors like mining and professional services held steady or even grew the total number of jobs on offer over the same period.[16]

Employers in the retail, hospitality and service sectors deal with this variability by hiring their staff on a casual basis. That means bosses can simply cut back hours or stop offering shifts altogether if business is slow. They also have little disincentive to lay off casual staff as it costs them nothing in redundancies or entitlements. Figures from the Australian Bureau of Statistics show that 65 per cent of people working in hospitality and almost 40 per cent of retail workers are casuals with no access to entitlements like sick leave or paid holidays. That's a huge chunk of the workforce, particularly when compared with sectors like banking, utilities and mining, where less than 10 per cent of workers are hired casually.[17] Collectively, we seem to have accepted this state of affairs as necessary to keep our shops and cafés going.

So the rise in underemployment and casual work among 20-somethings (and to some extent, higher unemployment) stems from a loss of those quality low-skill jobs that gave many of our parents their pathway into the job market. With those jobs gone, we are forced to gather instead in industries where work is less secure. Casual jobs in insecure sectors don't only come with fewer rights and conditions. They also offer fewer opportunities for skills development and career advancement. Young people who start their working lives here risk getting stuck in a cycle of insecure work as they grow older, watching mutely as better-trained workers move on and up. Our nation is not unique in this; almost every advanced economy is dealing with similar structural shifts in employment thanks to changing technology and globalisation. But as I'll argue in this book's final chapter, that doesn't mean we're powerless to tackle the inequalities this is creating.

The fact that young Australians are increasingly clustered in jobs at the cheap end of the service sector is also an important driver of the growing wage wedge between them and older workers. Here again, technology and globalisation matter. Over the past few decades, workers in professional and high-skill sectors like finance, law and IT have become much more productive. High-powered computers, the internet and instantaneous communication let them get a whole lot more done. At the same time, globalisation has greatly expanded the potential pool of demand for their skills. Where once a Melbourne finance guru might only have serviced customers in the CBD and surrounds, now plenty also have clients in Hong Kong, Jakarta or even further afield.

There simply has not been the same growth in productivity in the hospitality, retail or personal services sectors. It still takes roughly the same amount of time to pull a beer today as it did 30 years ago, and you can't ship a steak sandwich to Shanghai. One of the ways that the Australian Bureau of Statistics tracks the relationship between inputs and production is through its labour productivity index. Here, the difference between high and low service sectors could not be more apparent. Between 1989 and 2013, productivity in the financial and insurance services sector increased more than three times as much as that of the hospitality industry. The IT and communications sector boosted its productivity by almost 30 points more than retail did.[18]

Economics professor Jeff Borland from the University of Melbourne has estimated the value now produced by an hour's work across a range of sectors; not surprisingly, these professional sectors come out on top. He estimates that every hour a banker spends slaving over stock reports generates an average net value of $142. IT workers code their way to $93 in value per hour, while those running the cash registers at Myer generate only $34 an hour. Hospitality workers have the lowest productivity of all at just $31 an hour.[19]

So it seems that a big part of the growing wage gap between young people and those in later life can be explained by the different sectors they work within. Today's 20-something barista isn't much more productive than his

1980s predecessor. But a late-50s corporate lawyer is likely raking in far more cash for her firm now than in the past. We should hardly wish for some workers to become less productive again simply to reduce the wage gap between young and old. But neither should we treat this gap as inevitable or permanent just because it is caused by structural shifts that have been a boon for some. Working conditions are set by people making policy decisions; they are not divinely determined by some hand of fate.

You can get away with pointing out that technology and globalisation are making it harder for young Australians in the workforce in most polite company. But there's a third factor at work here, and it's far more *déclassé* to discuss it: the collapse of union membership. Any explanation for the rise in casual work, underemployment and slower wage growth among young people *has* to include the fact that few of us are joining unions these days. As Jake Rosenfeld puts it: 'For generations, the labour movement has stood as the most prominent and effective voice for economic justice.'[20]

It takes only a few facts to see why unions matter in this story. In 2013, mean weekly earnings were $139 higher for those in a union than for those who didn't belong to one.[21] Nine out of 10 union members work in a job with paid leave entitlements, compared with just seven in 10 non-union members.[22] Say what you like about their internal politics and PR practices, but unions clearly still play an important role in getting a better deal for workers.

Union membership has collapsed across the board over the past 25 years as the drumbeat of neoliberal individualism has drowned out the strains of 'Solidarity Forever'. But membership has dipped particularly low among the young. In 1990, one in four people aged between 15 and 19, and one in three people between 20 and 24, were members of a union. By 2013, this had fallen to fewer than one in 10 for both age groups.[23] Over the same period, union membership dropped from just under half of all workers in their mid-to-late fifties to a bit over one in four. The drop-off in membership among the young is problematic because unions have traditionally done the most to help those workers with the least. The casualisation of work in the hospitality sector, the underemployment of retail workers, the low wages for service sector staff – these are exactly the kinds of problems that unions exist to tackle. But with such thin coverage on the ground, mobilising the people and resources for the fight has been near impossible. That's why we've seen only patchy pushback against the increasing use of dodgy contracting arrangements and other types of insecure work.

There are two very simple solutions to this. Young Australians need to realise that there's more to unions than the hard hat–wearing thugs that Liberal governments have painted them as, and start joining again. And unions need to act a little less like medieval clans and more like modern, democratic organisations so that young people can actually identify with their mission. As I'll describe later on, unions like United Voice get this. Some have recently made great strides by putting community organising back at the centre of their work. We'll need better and stronger unions like these if we're to wind back the current inequality between young and old in Australia's workforce.

*

There is never going to be a time when young people starting out in work enjoy the same wages, security and conditions as more mature workers. That's simply not how the job market works. But there *was* once a time – within my own lifetime – when the workplace gaps between young and old were far smaller than they are now. If we let the gaps explored in this chapter continue to grow unarrested, then young Australians may well end up as an underclass of workers. Insecure, unprotected and inadequately paid, teens and 20-somethings will be left looking on as the benefits of work increasingly accrue to their elders. Plenty will also find themselves stuck as they age, with a lack of skills and opportunities locking them into the precariat.

Getting into a good job is the first hurdle for young Australians looking to build stable, comfortable lives. Too many are already stumbling at it today. But even those of us who've cleared this obstacle aren't finding a sure run into successful careers. As I'll explore in the next chapter, that's because our path is being blocked by older workers who are hanging on like grim death to all the good seats at the table.

CHAPTER TWO

WORK (GETTING ON)

I first became aware of the 'grey ceiling' when I was working as a researcher at one of Australia's more self-important universities. At our faculty's weekly seminars, the white-haired professors would saunter in and sit around a stately boardroom table under pictures of their younger, dark-haired selves; photos taken 10 or 15 years before, when they had first taken up their professorships. I would study these sages under my eyelids and marvel at their implacable sense of entitlement. A great number hadn't had a new idea in at least a decade. They specialised instead in shoe-horning any new development in their field into the confines of their pet theory. Each had a spacious office made cramped by faded books and years-old undergraduate essays. All were as embedded in the place as the electrical wires and water pipes.

We sessional lecturers and tutors would file in behind them and perch on plastic chairs around the edges of the room – a truly accurate visual metaphor for our tenuous status. We camped out two and three to a room in bare offices with little more than a computer and a phone, a salvaged chair and a wobbly bookcase. Our contracts ran from semester to semester: 15 weeks' work and never the promise of any more. They paid us by the hour for lectures and by the word for marking; like factory piecework but for people with PhDs.

In the three years I worked there, just five full-time, permanent roles opened up in the academic ranks. A handful of my casual colleagues moved interstate to take up lectureships elsewhere, having miraculously made it through recruitment rounds where applicants outnumbered jobs by the hundred. Our tenured colleagues in their late 30s and 40s feverishly pumped out papers and pimped themselves out for grants in the hope of ascending up the academic pay scale – mostly to no avail. And all the while the professors sat on in their named chairs; going nowhere and ensuring no one under them could either.

This isn't a phenomenon unique to my former university. Australians are working longer today than ever before. Many of them have to: the global financial crisis erased a sizeable chunk of the wealth they'd planned to retire with. Others have just realised there's no reason to quit work at 55 when they're in good health and the alternative is a 20-year stretch watching *Touched by an Angel* in their trackies.

In 1992 fewer than one in 10 of those in the workforce were over 55; today around one in six workers are.[1] Having so many aged employees sticking around for so long is something genuinely new in the world of work. As business writer Ira Wolfe notes: 'For the first time in history, four generations are working side-by-side. This scenario isn't just a brief passing of the torch moment either. For as long as Baby Boomers and their predecessors decide to keep working, the multi-generational workforce is here to stay.'[2] The 2015 Intergenerational Report predicts the participation rate for people in their mid-to-late 60s will rise from less than 20 per cent today to more than 50 per cent by 2055.[3] That's going to create much more competition for tomorrow's senior jobs.

We've been hearing an awful lot recently about the important contribution these older workers can make. The Intergenerational Report spruiked the increase in people working past traditional retirement age as 'a significant opportunity for Australia', with workplaces set to benefit from 'the wisdom and experience' of more aged personnel. That may well be true.

But having more people working into their 60s and beyond also comes at a very real cost to younger Australians. In earlier years, our parents' generation moved steadily through pay rises and promotions as people filed out of work at 55 and freed up the ranks above them. But having got old themselves, they're not giving up on those great careers. That leaves me and my peers butting up against a grey ceiling that compresses our potential and frustrates our ambitions. Worse, it may well see us earning less throughout key periods of our working lives.

NOBODY UNTIL YOU'RE AN OLD BODY

Pick a field – any field – and it's likely you'll find the age of its most senior people has risen compared with 20 or 30 years ago. The Australian public service? The average age of departmental secretaries for the eight most significant government departments has trended up by five years since 1990 alone – from 53 to 58.[4] In 1986, six of the key departments were headed by someone under 50; in 2014 not a single one was.

Big business? Taking a sample of Australia's biggest firms shows that their CEOs are, on average, eight years older now than 25 years ago.[5] In 1991 there were as many CEOs under 50 in this group as there were over that age, and just one senior executive was over 60. By contrast, in 2014 there were only five corporate bigwigs under 50 but three whose most recent birthday had a six in front of it.

The media? Editing newspapers has always been a younger man's game than running government or a big business. But even in this industry, the average age of the editors of Australia's major metropolitan newspapers trended up from 44 in 1990 to 51 by the end of the 2000s. A spate of younger hires like the *Australian*'s Clive Mathieson and the *Adelaide Advertiser*'s Sam Weir have caused that average to fall slightly again in the past few years. But those deciding the daily news are still three years older, on average, than their counterparts a quarter of a century ago. And don't get me started on the ossified artefacts of the (apparently) glorious 1980s who take up the majority of the opinion inches in our daily papers ...

FIGURE 4: AGE IN SENIOR ROLES 1990–2014

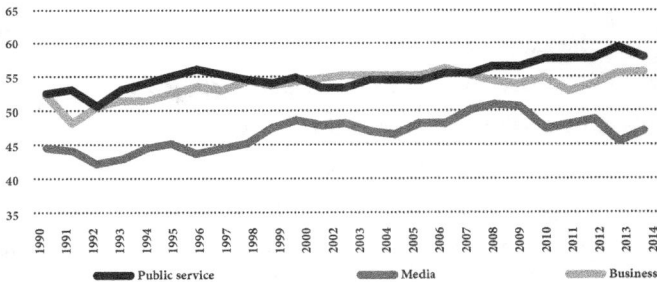

Data: compiled from public sources including Who's Who, news reports and company websites

Even Australia's political decision-makers are getting older. In 1983, Bob Hawke staffed his first ministry with spry types like John Dawkins (36), Paul Keating (39) and Susan Ryan (41). The average age around his cabinet table was 47. Twenty years later, the youngest members of Tony Abbott's first cabinet were 43-year-olds Peter Dutton and Mathias Cormann. The average age in his ministry as a whole was a more mature 53.[6] The membership of the federal parliament itself is also older than it was in Hawke's day. The average age in the House of Representatives has jumped from 47 to 55 between the 33rd and 44th Parliaments. (This, even despite the 2013 federal election bringing in a record number of 30-something parliamentarians.)

All this strongly suggests that today's workers have to wait longer to gain promotion to senior jobs than in the past. But since most of us will never rise to be a CEO, an MP or a departmental secretary anyway, does that matter?

Unfortunately for any 30-something seeking promotion, the data shows this age lag isn't confined to the top talent. For example, the Australian Public Service Commission puts out detailed data on the age and pay grade of all federal employees. Sifting these numbers shows people over 50 have dramatically expanded their share of mid-to-senior level roles over the past 15 years. At the same time, workers in their 30s and 40s have seen their representation shrink back.

The Executive Level 2 (EL2) band is a good place to look – it's the top general staff level before shifting into the senior executive. It is also the highest pay grade that most federal workers can realistically rise to; there are presently almost five times as many staff working at this level as in the entire senior executive.[7] Between 2000 and 2014, the number of EL2s aged over 50 jumped by more than 10 per cent. Over the same period, the number of people working at this level in their 30s and 40s went backwards by almost exactly the same figure.[8]

It's true that as proportionate shares of the population, there are more people over 50 around these days than in the 1990s, and slightly fewer people in their 30s and 40s. That's a result of the post-war baby boom, which was followed by falling fertility.[9] So we'd expect to see some change in the proportions of people holding senior jobs even if there was nothing else going on. But demographics alone don't account for the *scale* of change we've seen in Australia's workplaces. Instead, the career gains for older workers are being stripped from younger ones. Unless you believe Australians under 40 have become radically less promotable in the past 15 years (more on that in a minute), this should strike you as unfair.

Equivalent data for the private sector is hard to pin down. But given we've seen the same steady rise in age among Australia's big business and media chiefs, it's likely this is also happening among their Indians. This trend seems pretty inevitable if people are retiring much later than they used to. But it affects younger Australian workers in three unfortunate ways.

Most obviously, it hampers our careers because it shuts off opportunities for us to get promoted. If a couple of those professors at my old uni had shuffled off to be insufferable elsewhere, the middle-aged academics below them could have risen to take their place. This, in turn, would have freed up jobs all the way down the hall to those sparse offices where my temp colleagues and I clustered. But by staying put, those scholars stopped us all in our tracks.

Now, I can practically hear the screeching of senior workers as I type those words.

'Wait your turn, you tiresome brat.'

'Nobody handed us a good career on a plate.'

'We slogged our guts out for years to get to the top.'

Past generations did slug their guts out, and good on them. But here's the difference. Until fairly recently the workforce was like an escalator – lifting people steadily from their ground-floor jobs to the upper career echelons. Within a decade or two of stepping on that moving staircase, a sales assistant would become an area manager; a copywriter would be made an executive; a teacher would transition to principal. Former Treasury Secretary Chris Higgins was 46 when he was put in charge of the country's coin in 1989. Financier David Murray was running the Commonwealth Bank before his 44th birthday in 1992. The colourful journalist Col Allan was just 40 when he was made editor of the *Daily Telegraph* in 1993. Climbing so high by that kind of age is almost unheard of for today's workers, as the escalator increasingly flattens out to a treadmill.

On current trends, the wait for our turn at the top will on average be a decade or more longer than that experienced by our parents and grandparents. Our middle years will likely be spent in roles they would have looked down on at the same age. We don't expect sympathy from our elders for this. But neither should they expect silence from us while our career aspirations are being steadily strangled.

Frustrated ambitions aside, a scarcity of promotions also means more years working for crappier pay and conditions. In the last chapter I pointed out that average incomes for people in their 20s have grown at less than half the rate of that for people in their mid-fifties since

1990. They've also grown 16 per cent more slowly for people in their early and middle 30s.[10] That's likely to be because fewer of the workers in this bracket have moved from entry-level to better-paid roles than were able to do so in the recent past.

Even a few years' delay can have big financial consequences. For instance, a worker who spends an entire decade earning $60,000 will make $50,000 less in that time than one who gets a pay rise to $70,000 after five years. As I discuss in the next chapter, that difference represents a good chunk of what you need for the deposit on a median-priced house these days. The stuck-in-place shmuck will also pay thousands of dollars less into their superannuation during the years when saving for retirement does the most good. As I'll shortly show, younger Australians are facing an uphill battle to build the same kind of wealth that past generations did in their 20s and 30s.

Finally, there's the perception problem. As the number of sexagenarians in the senior grades grows, age is increasingly viewed as a prerequisite for holding those roles. When everyone around the boardroom table is pushing 70, someone in their 40s starts to seem under-qualified and immature (at least to those fogies choosing another for their ranks). It's the same problem that women have been facing for decades as we've tried to crack male bastions in business, politics and elsewhere. Younger workers are seen as lacking 'the right stuff' simply because we aren't ancient.

The flurry of appointments by the Abbott government in its first few years is a classic case in point. The government picked 76-year-old Maurice Newman to head the Prime Minister's Business Advisory Council. Tony Shepherd, 69, was tapped to head the National Commission of Audit. Dick Warburton was put in charge of reviewing the Renewable Energy Target at 72. *Crikey*'s Bernard Keane listed more than a dozen similarly aged appointments, sniping: 'See if you can spot a pattern.'[11] Was there really no one under 50 who was suitably qualified to advise the government on slashing welfare and sacking the environment? Of course there was. But they wouldn't have brought the wrinkled gravitas we're coming to expect from our grand poobahs.

I know what the response will be to all this. The problem isn't the jobs pipeline – it's today's young workers. We're overly skittish and sensitive. We're not prepared to stay put in one job for more than a year or two. Our expectations are too high and our taste for hard work too low. Media doyenne Kirstie Clements provided what may well be the definitive work in this canon with a piece published in Sydney's *Sun-Herald*. In it, she moaned about the 'extraordinarily entitled behaviour in the workplace by a generation that thinks hard work and respect for seniority are optional'.[12] Today's young workers, she griped, 'have difficulty separating confidence and self-promotion from delusion, especially in the digital space. They see no need for groundwork [or] time spent at the coalface ... we are now dealing with young adults who all won a prize at school simply for turning up, and who assume a career trajectory that includes having your job within the next 12 months.'

It's stirring stuff, but there's one small hitch: this is all little more than feelpinion that has assumed the status of fact.

GENERATION GENERALISATIONS

For a start, let's knock on the head this idea of my generation being unusually restless job-hoppers. At the moment, about a quarter of people between 20 and 34 change jobs in any given year. That sounds like a lot, and it's certainly higher than the one in eight 50-somethings who do so.[13] But when you drill down into the data, it turns out that this churn rate is actually *lower* than in the past. The local data on this goes back as far as 1993; then, one in three people under 24 had changed jobs in the past year. The proportion of those doing so in their late 20s and early 30s was almost exactly the same as today.[14] In the USA, labour force figures go back a decade further. They show that the proportion of young people changing jobs in any year has essentially been static since Reagan was president.[15]

People under 30 stay with each employer for a relatively brief 20 months – that has consistently been so since my parents entered the workforce in the late 1970s. The real shift in work habits these past few years has actually been among older Australians. Where people over 45 once averaged almost 10 years in a single job, today this is down to a bit more than six and a half years. Across the workforce as a whole, the average Australian employee now stays three years and four months before moving on to fresh fields. As the demographers at McCrindle Research point out: 'Young people have always had shorter job tenure than older workers, moving in and out of education, career changing [and] upskilling ... what is unique today is that the bulk of the workforce is following the lead of young people.'[16] In other words, if employers are concerned about shortening job tenures, it isn't us they should be dissing.

When it comes to attitudes and behaviours at work, serious studies find only limited and contradictory evidence of real differences between today's young and the old. There's no shortage of woolly focus group reports and management magazine surveys pointing to generational divides at the office. But proper peer-reviewed research gives cause to doubt whether there's anything more than daylight between workers at different ages.

For example, one study looked at how over 8000 workers of different ages conducted themselves during the workday. People in their 20s turned out to be a little less diligent than those in their 50s about showing up for work regularly and dressing and acting appropriately – but only slightly so. There was no difference between the oldest workers and the youngest ones on measures of conscientiousness, like being willing to work overtime when asked.[17]

Attitudes are where the generational differences are really supposed to bite. The stereotype is that today's young workers expect the penthouse suite moments after walking in the door. We don't believe we should have to do much to earn it, and we'll tantrum like toddlers if we don't get it. But when Emma Parry and Peter Urwin pooled the conclusions from 17 different studies of worker attitudes, they found a mess of conflicting outcomes. Some suggested that younger people are more status-conscious than older workers, while others reckoned all workers put equal stock in influence and responsibility. One group of studies found 20-somethings were motivated most by opportunities for self-enhancement and intellectual stimulation; another found it was all about cold hard coin. After due consideration, Parry and Urwin ruled that it is near impossible to tell if there's any truth in the lazy tropes about today's young workers on the basis of current evidence.[18]

Despite the lack of evidence, the perception that my generation don't make good workers is widespread, and it is damaging. It provides a convenient excuse for not promoting younger Australians into more senior roles. What's more, it lets older workers feel justified in keeping these to themselves, and paints our inability to get ahead as purely a product of our own failings. It's a cosy little cycle of blame and post-facto justification older generations are perpetuating. It's time we started calling them on it.

CUI (SHOULD) BONO?

The fact that older workers are changing the structure of the Australian workforce raises a tricky ethical question. Who has the stronger claim to the advanced jobs I've been talking about in this chapter? Or to put it another way, whose needs should take priority?

Viewed from one angle, there are good arguments for encouraging older workers to clear off and let others have a go. For example, in financial terms a promotion and pay rise brings much more benefit to a younger worker than a few more years in the job does to an older one. As I pointed out earlier, a pay bump in your 30s can mean the difference between buying a house (and so setting yourself up to grow wealth over time) or not. Today's older Australians have already acquired significant wealth – as we'll shortly see. So giving younger people access to the first building blocks for financial security could be seen as more important than ensuring those near retirement have the chance to stash away further thousands in superannuation.

There is also an intrinsic fairness argument here. Why should current and future generations be denied opportunities that were available to our elders simply because we were born later? Why should our skills and qualifications be devalued because of unfavourable demography?

Of course, viewed from another perspective, today's 50-something EL2s and over-60 CEOs have earned their stripes. They put in decades of hard work, rode out the turbulence through a period of unprecedented change and have often shown their organisations a loyalty that is now all but extinct. Asking them to forfeit these jobs would mean stripping healthy, switched-on people of intellectual and social stimulation as well as their daily purpose. What's more, the cost to the public purse would likely increase if tens of thousands more seniors were no longer working to support themselves.

You can see what I mean about this being an ethical bind for policymakers. We who are young and frustrated have good reasons for wanting the obstacles to our advancement cleared away. They who are old can make sensible, logical arguments for staying right where they are. Sometimes doing nothing is the best way to handle a dilemma like this. But in this case, doing nothing means coming down on the side of Australia's aged workers by default.

*

Some years ago now, Ryan Heath wrote the charmingly titled book *Please Just F* Off, It's Our Turn Now*.[19] In it, Heath made a case for Millennial exceptionalism, suggesting older Australians should make way for today's young because we are cleverer, more tech-savvy and more socially conscious than any previous generation. He stopped short of suggesting compulsory culling for over-50s who won't get out of our way – but only just.

It isn't only Heath who makes this argument – I've heard it from the mouths of almost every friend around my age over the past few years. You might find it hard to believe, given my throbbing antipathy towards my greying professors, but I disagree with Heath at both ends of his argument. For a start, there's nothing exceptional about today's younger workers. As I've shown, we're no worse than our elders – but I don't believe we're any better either. We're just another generation of Australians trying to build successful careers like those who came before us. It's frustrating to start cracking our heads on the grey ceiling precisely *because* we're the same as our forebears. Our skills and capabilities haven't changed, but the value attached to them has been deflated by the happenstance of demography.

I also disagree with the argument that older workers should 'just f* off' so we can have a turn at the top sooner. Yes, it's gallingly unjust that our careers should be stifled by our parents and their peers staying on in work longer. But it would be just as unfair to expect them give up jobs they've worked hard for, value and enjoy. Shifting hardship from one group to another doesn't make it go away. We should be wary of this kind of zero-sum zealotry if our goal is to build a fairer Australia overall.

It'll be worth you and me both remembering that as we shift the focus from work to the even pricklier topics of wealth and debt in the coming pages.

CHAPTER THREE
WEALTH

I don't own a house. I did, briefly. But my stint as a member of the propertied class ended when, at 28, I decided life as a suburban wife and mother was exactly as airless as Betty Friedan had described it. I left the house, and the husband with it, and fled back to a rented flat in the inner city.

We'd only been able to buy the place because a 'confirmed bachelor' uncle of my ex's had died and left him an unexpected lump sum. Even then, the best we could do was a falling-down 1970s three-bedder in the northern backblocks of Canberra. The sort of suburb where you'd more readily find meth than méthode traditionnelle at the local shops. I won't pretend I was all that sad to leave the house, at least, behind.

So now I am back among the 55 per cent of people aged 24 to 35 who bed down in the negatively geared nest eggs of grey-haired investors.[1] Thirty years ago, I'd have been in the minority to be renting at my age. Today, you have to stretch well into the late 30s age bracket before you find more than half of the group owning their own home.

Sitting on a pile of bricks isn't the only way to store up wealth throughout your life. But it's certainly how my parents and many generations before them became prosperous. Owning property is an investment, a source of collateral for new borrowing and a retirement plan rolled into one. Buy a house early in life and you're pretty much set – the market will cultivate your wealth for you as you go about your days. Buy later or not at all, and your financial future starts looking a lot less comfy.

In the 12 years since I first moved out of home, ownership rates among young Australians have plummeted. They are still falling as the price of property edges up and up. As I discuss in a later chapter, this directly affects the choices we make about partnering up, pushing out kids and putting down roots. Just as importantly, my generation's inability to get into the property market early is going to have lifelong repercussions for the wealth that we accrue. Those coming up after us will be even more financially dispossessed unless we act to rebalance skews in the system that favour their propertied elders.

In talking about wealth, it is also essential to give space to that least sexy source of capital creation: superannuation. Our current super system gives the most to those who already have the most, and it is failing to set young Australians up for the changed financial future we'll face. Recent policy choices by government have only widened the gap between those who benefit and those who fall behind in our super system.

I want to premise this part about wealth by saying one thing. Young Australians are often criticised for pissing our wealth away on overseas holidays and the latest Apple consumables. Demographer Bernard Salt believes today's young people simply have unrealistic expectations: 'They are the Gimme generation saying "I've got my Gameboy and iPod – where's my house? I am entitled to it . . ."'[2] Syndicated bores like Salt seem to believe that if we only buckled down and saved like our parents did, we would have all the same things they secured for themselves.

That simply isn't true. In the early 1980s, my newly married parents dutifully put aside one-tenth of their monthly income. At the end of just one year, they had enough of a nest egg to put down 10 per cent on a brand new three-bedroom house. Today, I could put aside the same share of my pay and at the end of a year I'd have less than one-third of the deposit for a studio flat in a far-distant suburb.

My point? It's not that young people spend because we don't know how to save. We spend because saving doesn't seem like it will get us anywhere. We spend because years of scrimping to buy a draughty weatherboard or a house and land package an hour from the city just isn't worth it. We spend because the gains of saving are too far on the horizon and moving ever further out of reach, no matter how many sandwiches we bring from home or concert tickets we forgo.

When it comes to accruing wealth over our lifetimes, we're not looking for a special leg up. Just having the same opportunities that let our parents and grandparents prosper would be a damn good start.

THE WORTH LESS

It's usually good to stand out somehow. Being different is a mark of distinction. But there's one factor that sets my friends and me apart from other Australians, and frankly, I'd rather it didn't.

Since 2004, the Australian Bureau of Statistics has been monitoring the average net worth of people at different stages through the life cycle. That's the dollar value of what they own after all debts and liabilities are taken into account. Adjusted to constant dollars, household net worth for people aged 15 to 24 grew by just under $30,000 in the not-quite-decade between 2004 and 2012. People in their mid-50s and early 60s saw their net worth grow by almost $179,000 – a respectable bump in anyone's book.[3]

But my cohort? We went backwards. Those aged 25 to 34 were worth $15,000 *less* in 2012 than people the same age in 2004. There's a good reason I still make my folks pick up the bill when we go out to dinner. The unspoken compact that children will enjoy more prosperous lives than their parents is breaking down, and that break starts with us. If you want further evidence, consider this: between 2004 and 2012 people in every age bracket over 45 saw their net worth *grow* by more than the *total wealth* of those under 25.[4]

FIGURE 5: NET WORTH BY AGE

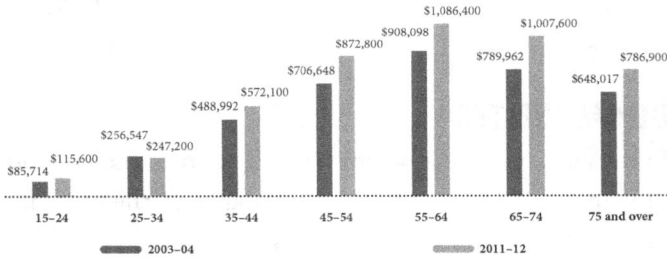

$1,086,400
$1,007,600
$908,098
$872,800
$789,962
$786,900
$706,648
$648,017
$572,100
$488,992
$256,547
$247,200
$115,600
$85,714

| 15–24 | 25–34 | 35–44 | 45–54 | 55–64 | 65–74 | 75 and over |

2003–04   2011–12

Data: Australian Bureau of Statistics, Household Income and Income Distribution Australia, cat: 6523.0

What's more, the gap in wealth between young and old has widened out by hundreds of thousands of dollars, as the figures below clearly show.

FIGURE 6: THE GROWING WEALTH GAP

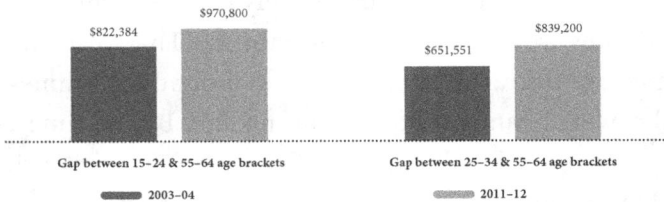

$970,800
$822,384
$839,200
$651,551

Gap between 15–24 & 55–64 age brackets   Gap between 25–34 & 55–64 age brackets

2003–04   2011–12

Data: Australian Bureau of Statistics, Household Income and Income Distribution Australia, cat: 6523.0

As the Grattan Institute's John Daley and Danielle Wood point out, the price of housing plays a huge role in this story of widening wealth gaps.[5] It almost single-handedly explains why my cohort has gone backwards compared with people in their late 20s and early 30s a decade ago.

GIMME SHELTER

In the past, most Australians had acquired a home by the time they hit my age. Even just 15 years ago, the majority of people in their late 20s and early 30s lived in a property they were paying a mortgage on.[6] But in 2012, just four in ten of my peers had managed to find their way into the property market.[7]

The reason for that is obvious to anyone who's scanned Domain recently: property is bloody expensive, and becoming more so all the time. My housing history tracks the story of its growing unaffordability all too neatly.

Mum and Dad bought my childhood home in 1982, building it from scratch in a freshly gazetted suburb 15 minutes from the centre of Canberra. That year, the median Australian house price was around three times the average annual household income. By the time I packed up my highly curated collection of '70s glam-rock albums and moved out of home in 2003, median prices had risen to about six times average incomes.[8]

In 2012, the year my then-husband and I bought our horrid house, the median price across Australia's six capitals hit $535,080, almost seven times the average income for people our age.[9] A flat would have been slightly more affordable – a relative bargain at five times average incomes for people like us. But those were the buoyant days when I imagined our home would soon be filled with crawling babies and boisterous toddlers. The thought of cramming all that human activity into an apartment was enough to bring me out in a cold, claustrophobic sweat.

Property has been a solid source of wealth creation for every Australian generation since Governor Macquarie parcelled out land that didn't belong to him. But those who already owned a home before the boom of the last 25 years have seen their wealth grow in ways that would have Trotsky reaching for the accelerant and wicks.

Between 1990 and 2013, the median price for all property across Sydney rose by $339,000 – a 262 per cent hike.[10] Properties in the suburbs closest to the CBD saw their median price jump by $555,000, a sum that would be eye-watering even if it was the base purchase price. My own parents banked quite the bounty when they finally parted with our family home a few years ago. Plenty of other 50-somethings I know are still squatting atop their appreciated assets like Smaug, breathing fire at anyone who suggests they might put their million-plus windfall to some more productive use.

It's hard to begrudge people like Mum and Dad the bump in wealth they've enjoyed through the recent property boom. They were assiduous about saving in their newly married days, lashed themselves to the mast to weather the interest rate storms of the early 1990s, and now know a financial comfort that would have been unimaginable to them in their youth. But what I cannot stomach – and what younger Australians should not stand for – is the persistent effort by propertied people to pull that ladder up after themselves. The extreme price of housing today is a direct result of state and federal government policies that suppress supply while feeding demand. The pressure put on governments to keep these policies in place should be seen as nothing less than Australia's old hoarding its wealth from the young.

Unlike many wicked policy problems, the causes of the current housing affordability mess are pretty clear. Too few homes are being built, and our tax system offers incentives that fuel an orgiastic desire for investment properties. Between 2001 and 2011, Australia's population grew by 15.9 per cent while our national housing stock increased by just 15.2 per cent.[11] As economist Saul Eslake has pointed out, that's a major shift from the post-war decades when new houses were being built much faster than people were being born to fill them. Even in 1982, when my parents were drawing up plans for their first place, Australia's housing stock was still growing about 1 per cent a year above population growth.[12] Modelling by the Housing Industry Association forecasts that we'll need to build 186,000 more homes each year between now and 2050 just to keep up with population growth – or around 15,500 a month.[13] Worryingly, over the past decade we've only been building new homes at an average rate of 13,800 a month.[14] If that continues, we'll fall over 20,000 houses behind each year as Australia's population continues to expand.

Then there's negative gearing, a policy so divisive that it makes parting the Red Sea look piss-ant. The idea that you can claim losses from one source of income as a tax deduction against another is perfectly fine in theory. But when owning a loss-making investment property or two offers a way to shrink your income tax bill, then you have a recipe for unhealthy demand.

In 2012–13 – the most recent year for which figures are available – just under 2 million Australians declared rental income to the tax office. But those landlords were clearly not so hot at property management, because only 706,000 of them declared a net profit on their rentals. In other words, a little more than six in ten Australian landlords were running their properties at a loss.[15] What would be disaster in business was actually a bonanza for them, as it allowed those owners to claim almost $42 billion worth of rent-related tax deductions that year. So Australia's landlords knocked an average of $21,500 off their tax bills by hoarding the country's housing stock.

Even with this tax perk, running a rental property at a loss still wouldn't make a lot of sense if it weren't for the capital gains tax discount introduced by the Howard government in 1999. This halved the amount of tax that owners pay on their profits when they sell an investment property.[16] As a result, you can use a rental to cut your tax bill for a number of years while that property increases in value. Then you make out like Midas when you sell, because the taxman expects a much smaller share of the yield than if you were earning regular income. It is this interaction between negative gearing and the capital gains tax discount that is widely seen as creating more demand than Australia's housing market can currently meet.

There's little data out there on just who owns all these loss-leading rental properties. But ABS figures show that in 2012, over 55s had an average of $53,000 in debt to their name for property loans that weren't on their primary residence. People under 35 had a little over $30,000 in equivalent debt while those under 24 held just $8300 on average.[17] This suggests it isn't primarily young people who are feathering their financial beds through this lucrative tax lurk. More tellingly, in real dollars over 55s more than doubled the average amount of money owed on properties they didn't live in between 2004 and 2012. By contrast, the figure for under 24s was almost flat. Some of that bump would be due to the price of boutique one-bedroom investment apartments rising alongside other house prices. But it also suggests that many more grey Australians have got into the negative-gearing game over the past decade.

Plenty of countries allow negative gearing, and the principle applies much more broadly than just to property in Australia's tax law. But we are one of the only countries in the world to allow rental losses to be deducted against *any* type of income. Many other places have determined that deductions can only be claimed against losses from the *same class* of income. In the United Kingdom, Canada and much of Europe, for example, you can reduce the tax owed for one profit-making investment property with deductions on a loss-making one. You can also carry over losses from one property year to year to cut your capital gains bill when you eventually sell. But you can't use the losses from your rented terrace to cut down the tax due for your day job, and capital gains still tend to be taxed at the payer's regular rate.[18] That means in other countries it simply isn't that practical to buy an investment property unless it makes a profit day to day. In its famously po-faced style, the Reserve Bank has observed that Australia's current policy set-up creates 'an unusually strong desire by existing property owners for further exposure to residential property.'[19]

When there are lots of people bidding to buy a limited number of properties, prices go up (and up, and up). And when some of those people have the security of property ownership behind them while others have nothing but a bare-minimum cash deposit, it's an easy bet who'll come off best in that bidding war.

The high cost of housing doesn't mean people buying a first home are priced out of the market altogether. As finance journalist Michael Pascoe points out, first homebuyers currently account for up to a quarter of all property pur-chases.[20] But what it does mean is that younger Australians are having to wait longer to buy while we scrape together a vast deposit. This fact shows up clearly in the data on where we're living at different ages.

Up until around the turn of the millennium, Austral-ians generally rented for their first few years out of home before buying in their mid-20s. In 2001, less than half of those aged 25 to 34 were still living in a rented home. This tipped the other way around 2007, when the proportion of renters in that age bracket jumped up to 54 per cent; it has stayed above half ever since.[21] Overall, almost 10 per cent fewer people now own a home by the time they reach their mid-30s than in 2001; ownership in this age bracket is down 25 per cent since my parents first bought.[22] If you break that figure down by income, the decline is even more marked. For the poorest young Australians, home ownership rates have crashed from 60 per cent to just 30 per cent over the past 15 years.[23]

Buying a home at 35 instead of 25 has lifelong conse-quences. For starters, it likely means at least a decade longer paying off a mortgage as you age. The average Australian mortgage is around $461,000 – a sum that would take two people paying 20 per cent of average wages almost 20 years to repay, even before factoring in interest.[24] Take out that mortgage at 25 and you can potentially be debt-free before you're 50, while owning an asset that has jumped in value to boot. But wait until your mid-30s or later and you'll still be paying that mortgage when you start planning your 60th birthday party. The former Labor government sparked a backlash when Wayne Swan announced Australia's official pension age would rise to 67 by 2023. The idea of retiring then is going to seem quaint to my generation, because many of us will still *have* to work to pay off the mortgages hanging over our silvered heads.

Not having property to your name is also problematic if you want to start a business or do anything else that requires major borrowing. Building your own company or investing in someone else's idea is another way that Australians like my dad have increased their wealth over time. As business expert Jeff Haden puts it: 'If you hope to get really rich, working for someone else will never get you there ... the only way to get really, really rich is to start your own business.'[25] Starting a business is inherently risky, which is why entrepreneurs tend to do it in their late 20s and early 30s – a time when they have fewer commitments and less to lose.[26] But if a bank won't trust you with the seed money because you have nothing to secure it against, that source of wealth creation slips away too. I don't think this point comes up enough when talk turns to the social and economic impact of higher property prices.

So the problem isn't only that my generation has gone backwards in wealth because we're struggling to break into the property market. An equally pressing predicament is the fact that this will hobble our efforts to become financially secure over our lifetimes. I mentioned at the start of this book that there are a couple of factors that will likely see my generation diverge from others at similar life stages as we move through our years. There's no question that the collapse in housing affordability over the past 15-odd years is the most significant of these. Many of us will be more financially pressed than our elders at 35, 55 and beyond because of it; it's basically already too late to stop that happening. The real question now is whether we can find ways to bridge the wealth gap so that the generations coming up after us don't suffer the same fate.

Right now, I can't see a time when I'll ever be able to afford another house. In truth, I'm not sure that I want one. The idea of being anchored in place by bricks and lawn seems at odds with the need to go with the flow as work and society changes around me. But I do want a future that's financially secure for myself and my son. One where I have something to my name, and where financial ruin is further away than one serious illness or bout of unemployment. One where I'm not entirely beholden to the fiscal whims of government when I reach a pensionable age. I want to be able to see a path from where I am today in a rented home with a little more than $10,000 in the bank, to where my parents are in their comfortable retirement.

Finding ways to make housing more affordable for the young will have to be part of any effort to shrink the growing wealth gap across the ages. But given the political shit storm that would inevitably involve, we'll also need to get better at helping young people plan for a future where we don't necessarily have a home as a nest egg. Success on *that* score will stand or fall on the settings in Australia's superannuation system.

SUPER UNFAIR

In Australia's social safety net, giving the most to those who already have the most is – rightfully – pretty rare. Across programs like Newstart, the aged pension and disability support, the accepted social compact is that we should focus our resources on those who need them most. Yet for some reason, that compact breaks down entirely when we make policy decisions about superannuation. The Australian government currently spends about $30 billion a year in tax concessions linked to superannuation. Almost 60 per cent of those concessions – some $18 billion a year – go to the top 20 per cent of income earners.[27]

While that upside-down redistribution is going on, young people simply aren't storing away the kind of wealth we'll need in the future. That's partly because of the prevalence of insecure work and slow wage growth I talked about in Chapter 1. But it's also down to policy settings that skew the super system towards older and wealthier Australians. Fixing the former is a major challenge, but a few simple tweaks to our super rules would make the system much more equitable.

As with so many of the factors I've discussed, super saving follows a distinct trajectory over the life cycle. Young people have only a little set aside at the start of our careers as we begin making payments. This gradually grows over time into a healthy pile of coin ready to fund the cruises and fix the crook knees of our retirement. But just as we've seen bigger gaps opening up between young and old in work, wages and housing wealth, the relative size of super savings across the ages is also significantly pulling apart.

In real dollars, average super savings for people under 25 rose by almost $3500 between 2004 and 2012, hitting just under $15,000. Over the same period, people in my age bracket (25–34) saw average holdings increase by a little over $11,000. Older people did far better, with savings for people aged 45 to 54 jumping by $46,000, and those aged 55 to 64 holding $81,000 more in 2012 than people the same age in 2004.[28] That means the superannuation savings gap between young and old has widened out by $78,000 for people under 25, and by $70,000 for people in their late 20s and early 30s.

FIGURE 7: SUPER SAVINGS BY AGE

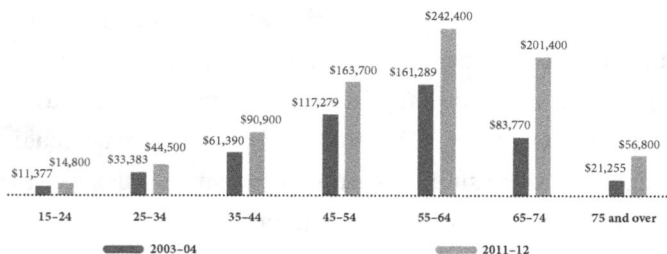

Data: Australian Bureau of Statistics, Household Income and Income Distribution Australia, cat: 6523.0

Because super automatically comes out of pre-tax wages, the type of work you do and how much you get paid for it has a direct impact on your savings. One big problem for young people is that casual workers are far more likely to see their super go underpaid or not paid at all by dodgy bosses. The Australian Taxation Office estimates that there is up to $1 billion in unpaid super owing to Australian workers, with casual workers in the cleaning, hospitality and retail sectors particularly at risk of getting ripped off.[29] As I pointed out in Chapter 1, over half of those under 25 now work in casual jobs. That means there's a big number of young Australians who simply never see the super they're owed.

I went back to check my own super statements for the years I worked in bars and cafés, and it's likely I can count myself among this number. Over five years of working around 15 hours a week, a back-of-the-envelope calculation says my bosses should have paid about $5600 into my super account. Yet when I left uni and finally snagged a full-time, permanent job, there was only around $3000 stored up in my fund. Somewhere along the way I got dudded big time. Unfortunately, amid the late nights and questionable boyfriends of that time, I didn't pay enough attention to my personal finances to notice.

Slower wage growth among the young also helps to explain why our savings are increasing at less of a clip than those of our elders. At the moment, an early-20s worker on the average wage adds about $85 a week to their super savings. But if wages for this age bracket had grown as fast as they did for 50-somethings over the past 20 years, they'd be adding $108 a week. An extra $22 doesn't seem like much on its own, but that adds over $1000 a year to total savings. Addressing the casualisation of work and slower wage growth among the young would improve our financial security both now and into the future.

Another reason why super savings have grown much more for the old than the young is that there are serious tax perks to be gained if you're a high-income earner who makes voluntary contributions. Super contributions are taxed at a rate of 15 per cent, while Australia's top marginal tax rate is 45 cents in the dollar. So storing money as super wins the wealthy a 30 per cent tax cut. This same advantage doesn't apply if you're already paying a much lower tax rate, as anyone earning around the median wage for under 25s would be. This imbalance prompted writer and social commentator Eva Cox to observe that: 'Superannuation tax concessions are a rip-off, as they give the largest benefits to higher income earners and little or nothing to low-income groups ... Australia's superannuation system functions as "rich people's welfare".[30]

In the lead-up to the 2015 Budget, there was a blaring chorus of calls for the government to do something about this blatant unfairness in the super system. Economics writer Peter Martin estimated that the treasurer could plug almost all of Australia's current budgetary hole simply by removing super tax concessions that favour higher earners.[31] And yet May came and went with no major changes to the tax treatment of retirement savings, prolonging for at least another year settings that benefit the older and better off.

Looking ahead to how the super system will work for today's young Australians, the Liberal government has made two decisions that will see savings growth shrink when we need it to increase. First, against all good advice, the government opted to delay a scheduled rise in the compulsory super contribution rate. The rate was supposed to rise in stages from 9.5 per cent in 2014 to 12 per cent by 2019. The government has now pushed out that timeframe to 2025, with no increases at all between today and 2021.

On top of pausing the super rate rise, the government is also phasing out the low-income super contribution scheme by 2017. This scheme puts up to $500 a year into the super accounts of people earning less than $37,000. Some 3.6 million Australians are eligible for the payment, a figure that would include almost every young person working casually or part-time. The scheme cost the Budget $975 million in the financial year 2013–14; less than one-thirtieth of the amount we spent on super tax concessions that same year.

The combined impact of these decisions on the young?

Industry Super Australia estimates that a 25-year-old who is earning the average wage today will have around $100,000 less in super savings when they retire than they would have without these changes.[32]

It is only fair to note that our current super system isn't preparing those already approaching old age that well for retirement either. The benchmark ASFA Retirement Standard suggest that a couple needs to have set aside between $620,000 and $1 million to live comfortably after leaving the workforce.[33] Worryingly, the average Australian bloke currently retires with only $197,000 in his super fund, while women are seriously lagging behind, with just $105,000 set aside.[34]

But at least most of those retiring in the next couple of decades will have houses they can sell to make up the shortfall. They've almost certainly seen those properties gain hundreds of thousands of dollars in value in the years since buying them. More likely than not, they'll own them outright by the time they're ready to retire. By contrast, I've currently got only about $35,000 in my super account and few assets bar the MacBook Air I'm writing this screed on. Without property – or with a mortgage that will stretch past the pension age – a shortfall in superannuation becomes a much bigger problem.

Our super settings are the product of policy choices. The design of the system is up to our government. The effects of their choices will ricochet down the decades and determine a lot about the wealth today's young people end up building over our lifetimes. Far fewer of us will have the financial fallback of home ownership as we age, but Australia's super system hasn't yet adapted to that new reality. Our first priority should be to scale back the super benefits given to those who need them least so that initiatives like the low-income super contribution scheme can be maintained. Then we need to look for new ways to fill the wealth gap younger Australians are facing.

*

I didn't grow up thinking I'd be Packer-wealthy as an adult. I didn't even expect sports-star-with-a-cereal-endorsement-contract level of comfort. If I'd had to say, at age nine or 15, what I thought my future would look like, I would probably have described a life a lot like what Mum and Dad had. A house big enough to tend teenagers in. A new car every five or so years. A regular but not-too-flash holiday rental near the beach over Christmas. Naturally, at nine I would also have said that future home needed its own tap floor and light rig; at 15, that crucifixion would be preferable to having any of those things in Canberra.

But I certainly believed the basic template of that life, with its steady accrual of wealth and stability, would be within my grasp by now. It isn't for me and many others my age, and that's a problem Australians across the years should be worried about.

If young and old pull apart in wealth, the end result can only be a less connected community. We joke about technology divides as we watch our grandparents come to grips with their iPhones and LOL at the culture gap for those over 50 who try to make sense of today's yoof slang. But wealth inequality creates real divides. It separates people across cities and opens fissures among their habits, tastes and interests. It breaks down understanding and creates jealousies. I won't lie – I already feel a hot twist in my stomach whenever I meet a 50-something with a tastefully renovated home and a newish car parked outside. I resent what they have because it is so much more than I'm likely to ever acquire.

Much more pragmatically, leaving young people to fall behind in wealth also works against the prevailing idea that we should be as financially independent as possible when we're old. The Intergenerational Report, the Murray Financial Systems Inquiry, the Tax White Paper – every official word from government says Australia can't afford to keep shelling out billions on pensions and services for a growing cohort of grizzled retirees. But if we can't start building wealth when we're young, we simply won't have enough of it not to rely on government when we're aged.

Improving housing affordability and rebalancing super savings will help shrink the wealth gap that has yawned open between young and old Australians. But no one gets wealthy when they're drowning in debt.

That's why we also need to stop young people digging deeper into the financial holes too many are wallowing in today.

CHAPTER FOUR
DEBT

I know a 24-year-old who has about $1000 dollars in credit card and store debt to his name for every year he's been alive. He pays the minimum couple of hundred each month to keep the banks from sending bailiffs to his door, but never manages to shift much of the principal. I asked him once how he plans to ever pay that debt off, given his current yearly salary is only slightly more than twice its size. He looked at me with that infuriating blank stare 20-something blokes excel at and shrugged.

Another friend lurched through three semesters of a Law degree before realising that 21 was probably a good age to stop pandering to her highly strung parents and make her own decisions. She now works in a day-care centre and half jokingly says that the crappy wage is worth being exempt from paying her $13,000 HECS debt. My own brother almost bankrupted himself taking out a titanic loan to buy a house by the beach in north Queensland. Even working in the mines and earning more than many corporate lawyers wasn't enough to keep in front of his repayments.

My own liabilities are nothing unusual in this company. A few thousand dollars across two credit cards – mostly books and clothes and Buy It Now ephemera from eBay. A car loan with about $5000 outstanding. A nauseating chunk of HECS debt that I hope to pay down now I've run out of degrees to add to the tab.

In the last chapter I discussed how young Australians are battling to build the wealth that insulates our olds, principally because of the high cost of housing and flaws in the superannuation system. The other side of that wealth story is debt, because today's 20-somethings are lugging more of it than ever. Huge house prices are again at the centre of the frame, putting those who manage to get into the market under heavy financial pressure. But rising education costs and the easy availability of credit are also part of the problem.

You won't find me arguing that debt is a bad thing. If we couldn't borrow, it would only be the swells with inherited wealth who would ever buy a home or start a business. But when today's young Australians are hauling a heavier debt burden than previous generations, that affects both our quality of life today and our financial prospects for the years ahead. A moderate amount of debt can be a positive. But too much of it leaves us frantically jogging on the spot financially or, worse, being sucked backwards.

MORTGAGED MORE

Having been on both sides of the property divide, I'm unsure which is worse. It does worry me that I'm steaming into my 30s without any concrete way of reinforcing my financial future. But during the brief few years that the ex and I *did* own a house, the thought of our piled debts never failed to cause me chest constrictions.

The place cost us almost $420,000, despite one end of the kitchen floor rising fully four centimetres above the other because the house was gradually sinking into the claggy yard. It faced the street with flaking wood-framed windows; once, an entire section of a frame came away in my hand as I reached out to stop myself falling down the front step. The ceiling in the hallway between the living room and our bedroom had a snaking crack almost wide enough to fit my index finger into.

Without the fabulous dead uncle's contribution, a 10 per cent deposit would have meant us finding over $40,000. Since the husband was running a café and I was teaching part-time to supplement a research scholarship, that figure was just under half our pooled yearly earnings. In the three years we'd been saving for a deposit before the unexpected payout, we'd only managed to put aside $15,000.

After we bought the house, monthly repayments ate up almost 40 per cent of all the money we had coming in each week. This, even at a time when interest rates were going through their post-GFC depressive phase. I bitterly resented that much money disappearing from our account when it never seemed to make the barest nick in the amount outstanding on the bank statement.

Everyone says buying your first home is hard. Everyone knows you have to take on a burden of debt to do it. But the quantum of that debt was vastly different for my parents and people in past generations. This gave them financial breathing room few young mortgagees feel today.

When my parents built their first home, the deposit set them back less than one-tenth of their annual income. That's not because they were earning a lot; Dad was a plumber and Mum left work to care for we three kids. Housing was just astoundingly cheap then by the yardstick we're used to today. Sure, interest rates were running at 12.5 per cent – a figure that would mortify most Millennial homeowners. But even with the high cost of borrowing, their monthly repayments demanded just one dollar in ten of my parents' combined income.

You can ask families across Australia and hear this story over and over again. As the Foundation for Young Australians points out, in 1985 the average home loan held by a first homebuyer was a bit over $81,000 in today's money. Today, that average has jumped to $308,000.[1] That much debt wouldn't be such a problem if other things were rising alongside it. Unfortunately, they're not. Average household debt stood at 40 per cent of annual income around my second birthday; by my 27th it had spiralled up to 180 per cent. In other words, the average Australian household now has debts that add up to 1.8 times their yearly income.[2] That's a higher debt ratio than in any other country we might like to compare Australia with, including the USA, UK, Canada, Germany and Japan.

The debts we hold have also grown far faster than the value of the assets we hold them against – about twice as fast, according to analysis from the Australian Bureau of Statistics.[3] People buying today are therefore unlikely to see anything like the huge returns enjoyed by home-owners over the past 20 years, because the cost of servicing such massive mortgages will mostly cancel these out. If you hold a $308,000 mortgage on a median-priced house, you'll pay about that again just in interest repayments over the course of a 25-year loan. So you're already up to over $600,000 before breaking even on the loan itself. Making the kind of profit that has feathered the retirement nests of my parents' generation would require property prices to keep growing well into the multi-million dollar range. That's unlikely to happen unless income growth picks up significantly, because at some point the market simply runs out of buyers who can afford to pay so much.

The excessive price of housing has created a drowned-if-you-do, starved-if-you-don't bind for today's young Australians. Those locked out of the property market are seeing the opportunities for long-term wealth creation recede. But those who can get across the threshold are suffering a huge hit to their disposable income now and into the middle distance, all for less gain than previous generations enjoyed.

That situation is only exacerbated by the fact my friends and I also have other debts that our parents were blissfully unencumbered by when they were still fit and firm.

A NEW CLASS OF DEBT

My mum was the first in her family to get a university degree. Not just the first among her five siblings and parents, but the first in her extended Irish Catholic brood of cousins, aunts and uncles as well. She had the good fortune to be leaving school just as Gough Whitlam came to power and abolished university fees. For 15 much-celebrated years between 1974 and 1989, bright kids who made the grades were able to get a degree for free.

Mum is in good company among that crop of Whitlam graduates. It includes a good number of the current government and Opposition frontbenchers, and the CEOs of many of the biggest companies in this country. It also includes many of the peak body shills who've recently lobbied hardest for 'budget reform' (i.e. massive spending cuts to things like tertiary education). But more on that in a moment.

When the Hawke government reintroduced uni fees, they were set at a flat rate of $1800 for all students, or just over $3500 in today's money. Successive policy changes during John Howard's prime ministership both increased fees overall, and created a tiered system where degrees that bring higher earning potential – think medicine and dentistry – cost more than arts degrees (which may as well come with Newstart forms attached).

The result is that today's medical student leaves university lugging around $50,000 in student debt, while the philosophy graduate leaves with about $18,000 on their ledger. Some young Australians, too, run up big HECS bills without ever completing their degrees. That's a double-down debt trap, because they leave university with a financial liability but lacking the qualifications that would help them get good work to repay it.

Given these policy changes, you won't be shocked to hear that the amount of education debt young Australians hold has doubled over the not quite decade between 2004 and 2012. Since older Australians have little or no education debt, the gap between them and the freshly graduated has also widened. In 2004 under-25s had, on average, $3400 more student debt than their olds; by 2012 this gap had risen to $6200.[4] That mightn't seem like much but it's important to remember that this is an average across the entire age bracket. Less than 40 per cent of school leavers go to university today,[5] so the debt gap between those who've been on campus in the past decade and those free-riding Whitlam graduates now in their 40s and 50s is actually far greater. The big jump in university fees during the Howard years is a second significant factor that will set Australians currently in their 20s and early 30s apart from previous cohorts. God help those coming after us if fees are increased further or deregulated entirely.

Education debt is a drag on those who hold it long after they've graduated. Modelling done by think tank Demos found that a couple with a combined $53,000 in student debt can expect to suffer an average wealth penalty of $208,000 over their lifetime.[6] That's because they'll spend more of their early-career disposable income repaying their student loans instead of putting that money into property or stashing it away as savings. The Treasury tells us that Australian students currently take about eight and a half years to pay off their debts, so most will only clear these before blowing out the candles on their 30th birthday cake.

Big student debts also have an impact on the cost of professional and other services for people who don't, themselves, have degrees. As the University of Adelaide's Andrew Beer points out: 'When graduates enter the workforce with bigger debts, they will demand higher wages to compensate.'[7] A solicitor with a significant education debt is going to charge higher fees to pay it down; a dentist isn't going to wield their drill on the cheap when they have bills to pay. Doctor and author Pauline Chen argues that the astronomical price of degrees in the USA is one important factor in the similarly high cost of services like medicine there.[8] There's little data available on how prices have already changed in Australia as a result of the university fee hikes throughout the 2000s. But it's something we should be keeping an eye on, because the affordability of legal, medical and other services has community-wide impacts.

I know it isn't feasible to return to the days of free degrees when two in five young Australians are now taking up seats in our halls of higher learning. But accepting that a degree must cost *something* is very different from contentedly watching on as students are saddled with ever-deepening debt.

I'm worried that higher education has become an area where governments look to make savings to offset the expected spike in pension and health costs for the aged. The Abbott government's (thankfully dumped) proposal to uncap fees while at the same time cutting university funding by 20 per cent is a recent case in point. Geoff Sharrock from the University of Melbourne has modelled possible outcomes from a policy switch like this. Note that Australian students already pay some of the highest tuition fees in the world, relative to wages and the cost of living.[9] Sharrock estimates that if fees were uncapped, student debt would rise by between $16,000 and $98,000, depending on just how much universities choose to hitch them up.[10] At the top end of the range, students would likely be paying off their HECS debts well into their 40s.

Egged on by a Greek chorus made up of voices like the Business Council of Australia and the Australian Chamber of Commerce and Industry, the government pitched these higher ed changes as a necessary part of the 'budget repair' task. This is pretty much equivalent to your parents saying, 'Sorry, kids, you'll have to fund your own school fees – Nana's hip operation isn't going to pay for itself'. As

Alan Tapper, Alan Fenna and John Phillimore have pointed out, there's actually a lot of this sort of redistribution from young to old now going on within our tax and transfer system.[11] Between 1984 and 2010 the net benefits[12] directed to people under 24 grew by $82 a week. Those over 65 saw a significantly bigger boost of $261 a week, even as the number of greysters in this age bracket exploded. At the same time, the weekly income tax take grew by $22 on average but shrank by $26 for over-65s specifically.

When young Australians are already paying it forward in our tax and transfer system, shifting more of the university fee load from government to students seems both unfair and bloody myopic. For one thing, it risks pricing some young people out of higher education altogether – particularly those from disadvantaged communities who would most benefit from the leg-up into work that a degree can provide. For another, the country as a whole benefits when we add to our ranks of highly skilled graduates.

Former education minister Christopher Pyne injected a note of anti-elitism into the higher education debate by pointing out that 'less than 40 per cent of the population have a university degree, so more than 60 per cent of the Australian public are paying 60 per cent of the costs of students to go to uni.'[13] The clear implication is that sub-urban battlers are unfairly subsidising the degrees of the book-learned elite.

Now, I don't know how Mr Pyne feels about amateur surgeons stitching up accident victims or untrained teachers helping kids learn to read. But I'm pretty sure the majority of Australians would prefer workers like these had a degree, and therefore see a collective value in higher education even if they don't personally partake. This is a rare case where what benefits some of us is also good for the lot of us. Loading up students with excessive debt is therefore bad for our community as a whole as well.

The scale of housing and student debt is largely out of young people's hands – it is set by the market and the government. But there is one other type of debt that also damages the financial standing of young Australians, and in this case we're mostly piling it on ourselves.

CREDIT WHERE IT'S DUE

My generation has a problem with credit. I won't pretend we don't. Long dead are the days my parents speak of, when furniture or tech would be paid off in fortnightly instalments before being paraded proudly home. Now anything you want is just a payWave away, and far too many of us are habituated to that swiping. House prices aside, the question of credit is the big fault line between today's young and our exasperated parents. They think we're a bunch of instant gratification addicts who lack the patience to save for things we want. I'd argue our relationship with credit is a mite more complicated than that.

Detailed information on credit liabilities and user habits is surprisingly difficult to come by. You can guarantee the banks themselves have it and can slice it any which way to the third decimal place. But damned if they're giving it out so that we can share the insights they have on our plastic habits.

ABS surveys seem to show that Australians owe only a moderate amount on credit and non-property, non-business loans, at $6100 for people under 24 and $8300 for people in their late 20s and early 30s.[14] That's not too far out of whack with the $5600 owed by people in their 50s, and all of those figures are actually lower than during the boom years of the early noughties. The global financial crisis taught many of us to be more wary of borrowing, and that can be seen in the amounts we have outstanding today.

But this age-bracket average is also a little misleading, since the Reserve Bank of Australia reckons no more than one in three people actually has credit card debt (in any age group).[15] Plenty of people can't afford to get credit, and some are wealthy enough not to need it. Then there's the fact that this doesn't capture in-store financing, like those infamous '18 months interest-free' loans at Harvey Norman, which attract a 30 per cent compounding interest rate if paid late. It also doesn't include things like mobile phone and cable plans. These are basically another form of credit, since you get to take your iPhone or iQ box home and pay for it in contracted monthly instalments. Young people seem to be much more enthusiastic clients of these particular lenders than older Australians.

But good numbers on just how this adds to our overall debt pile are frustratingly difficult to come by.

Our primary problem with credit is not necessarily the dollar value of it anyway. Instead, we're paying a hefty price for an inability to give back what we owe on time. In credit card circles, there are three kinds of customers.[16] The kind no bank wants too many of are known as *transactors*, those who pay off their entire balance every month. Banks make nothing from these customers, because they're conscientious about avoiding late payments and interest charges. My mother falls into this category: she has had a credit card since about 1980 and has never – repeat, never – failed to pay off the balance by the end of the month. That's a heroic feat of financial management that I am frankly in awe of.

The second category is *infrequent revolvers* (or 'sloppy payers', in the memorable description of one former banker I met). These customers mostly clear their balance on time, but will sometimes be a month or two late. Then there are *constant revolvers*, the fatted calves of credit companies. These customers rarely, if ever, pay off their full balance, and incur big interest charges from rolling it over month to month. I'm an incorrigible constant revolver. With two credit cards each charging 16 per cent interest, I've worked out this bad habit cost me almost $1000 last year.

I'm not alone in this failing. Consumer research from Roy Morgan found that Australians under 25 roll over an average of $2500 in credit card debt each month without paying it off.[17] When Nicki Dowling and her colleagues at Victoria University surveyed the financial habits of Melbournians in their late teens and early 20s, over 40 per cent said they rarely or never paid off their balance at the end of a month.[18] Fully half of those with credit cards also reported regularly maxing them out, which is a bit of a worry considering their average credit limit was around $4600. The major banks could no doubt shed a lot more light on just how big a problem this is for young Australians. But don't hold your breath waiting for that data to come out, since every 20-something's revolving balance helps grow their billion-dollar bottom line.

So yes, we have a problem. We rack up bills bigger than we can afford to pay off each month, and we really shouldn't. Don't think for a moment I'm trying to downplay the importance of personal responsibility in managing our money well. But there *are* some important social factors underpinning our relationship with credit. For a start, it is now crazily accessible and seemingly so cheap (until you read the fine print). Since the deregulation of Australia's banking sector in the 1980s, it has become progressively easier to get loaded up with plastic. One simple reason people in previous decades didn't run up as much credit is that few places were offering it to them. I really doubt my parents would have been such patient lay-by payers if they'd had the option to bring their booty home straightaway. But today we can get credit everywhere, with the bar set as low as: can you afford a few bucks for the minimum monthly repayments?

A couple of work and wealth factors also matter here. As I highlighted in Chapter 1, many more young people today are muddling through with work that is casual, insufficient or both. When that's the case, credit becomes a necessary stopgap for smoothing out gaps in the weekly budget and paying for big expenses that materialise out of the blue. My sense is that this leads to bad habits that are hard to kick as we get older. The weight of a few thousand in unpaid fees comes to feel unremarkable, which then makes adding to it relatively effortless.

One of the reasons I'm a constant revolver with my own cards is that a balance of $1500 feels paid to me. When it starts climbing to multiples of that, I'll cut back for a few weeks to pay it down. But as soon as it gets near that magic figure, all motivation to clear the rest suddenly vanishes. I only recently realised that amount is the maxed-out balance I maintained through most of my undergraduate years on the credit card my parents had set me up with 'for emergencies'.

There's also the inequality issue. My generation has been marinaded since birth in a want-it-buy-it-you-deserve-it culture that would make Sherman McCoy blush. That's because we've grown up in a time when Australia has become much richer overall, and a few have become prodigiously more wealthy than most. Australia's net national disposable income per capita rose from a little over $30,000 in the year I was born to more than $53,000 today.[19] As I've already described, inequality rose across the board during these years, and at the same time older people began breaking ranks with the young on their earnings and wealth.

When there's plenty of money in a community, there's also plenty of the nice stuff money buys: big houses, flash cars, sleek tech, gourmet foods. An Australian from the 1950s would be astonished at how visibly rich our country is today. That wealth isn't even close to evenly shared, but when I talk with my peers I'm often struck by the role credit plays in helping us live as if it is. We don't go without if we can't afford an iPad; we simply put it on credit. We won't make do with second-hand sofas and drooping bedframes; instead, we charge-card new ones. Our critics grouse that if we don't have the cash, we should go without, just as they did in their day. But when my parents were young – and certainly my grandparents – they weren't surrounded by people richer than them flaunting things that were out of their reach. Australia being less wealthy and more equal made for fewer visible distinctions in people's material possessions. I firmly believe my generation's constant exposure to wealth has warped our perspective on what the baseline for a good life is. For plenty of us, then, credit acts as a scaffold spanning the gap between our means and our unconscious expectations. It's yet another reason to care about inequality: because the 'haves' holding a conspicuous lot starts to distort the behaviour of the 'have-nots' before long.

Short of cutting up everyone's cards, I don't know what the solution to this credit conundrum is. So don't go looking for one in the final chapter when I talk about some of the ways we can help young Australians look to a less debt-burdened future overall. Making consumer credit a little *less* accessible by lifting the bar on lending criteria and minimum repayments would certainly help. So would better financial education in schools. But the inequality element and the need to top up insufficient take-home pay won't be fixed by tinkering with bank rules or schooling. These are bigger economic ills of which our credit dependence is merely a symptom.

*

Let me say one more time: debt is not, in itself, a bad thing. If housing could only be purchased in cash; if student fees could not be deferred to HECS; if everyone only had what they could pay for upfront, Australia would be a *much* more unequal place. Debt plays a very important role in ensuring those who aren't already loaded can start down the path to prosperity.

The problem we presently have is that young Australians carry too much debt relative to our incomings and the likely value we'll get out of it. My home-owning friends won't see more of a return for having mortgages nearly four times bigger than the ones on their childhood homes. In fact, they'll likely see far smaller returns than our parents pocketed in the last 15 years. My degrees haven't made me more employable or seen me earn a great premium over someone with these same qualifications 20 years ago. But they're certainly costing me more of my take-home pay each fortnight. Consumer credit has taken our short-term need for cash and turned it into an expensive, long-term liability on our personal balance sheets.

All this puts more barriers in front of young Australians looking to build prosperous lives like our parents have. But before we start talking about ways to solve these problems, there's one more important issue that must be stared in the face. Younger Australians are experiencing fading wellbeing as today's trends affect how we live, love and fit into the wider community. Spend time among people my age and it can sometimes start to feel as though being happy and content has become a perk reserved for others older than us.

CHAPTER FIVE
WELLBEING

In my late teens and early 20s I had a very dear friend who was into self-harm. The serious kind. She was beset by many anxieties and when things all got too much, she would drag a Stanley knife across her paper-white inner arms until they blossomed red. Her upper thighs were scarred like those of a Papuan Highlander too. She said the cutting felt like getting laid and lifting off in an airplane all at once. She said it felt like peace.

I think of her often when talk among my peers turns to the many pressures piling onto us today. As messed up as her chosen method was, I know plenty of under-30s who would identify with her desire for release. To be freed from the pressing weight overshadowing us, even if momentarily.

In the past few chapters I've talked a lot about how my generation is doing materially. Now, I want to do something deeply un-Australian and spend some ink on how we're going emotionally. Because young people are falling behind in our wellbeing just as much as in our workplaces and wealth creation. The world out there is darkening the domain inside our heads and dragging down our spirits.

And why wouldn't it? The globe is warming around us, yet governments stall on meaningful action to slow the process. Privacy and rights are slowly being sacrificed on the gilded altar of national security. Our state continues to sanction discrimination in love, that most basic expression of our humanity. Plunk meta-worries like these on top of the pressures I've already talked about in work and wealth, and unhappiness seems to me a rational response.

Wellbeing is closely tied to whether we can provide for ourselves and build stable, secure lives. But it is also linked to the quality of our relationships, the place we have in our communities and whether we feel heard in deciding the shared direction of our neighbourhoods, our cities and this country as a whole.

Today's young Australians lack much of the private scaffolding that supports wellbeing, like long-term partnerships, kids and community roots. Our elders disparage us as kidults determined to avoid real life for as long as possible, but they're wrong. The 'choice' to delay these milestones of adulthood is all-but unavoidable in the current environment. We are frankly tired of hearing that we're feckless, reckless and failing at life when we're already paying an emotional price for the instability of our circumstances.

Very often, too, we feel that our views don't matter, as though our priorities never make it to the top of the national to-do list. As I'll show in this chapter, young Australians depart from the old in our opinions and preferred course of action on a range of really important national questions. Yet the booming voices of people in their 50s and 60s continue to talk over us and tamp down progressive change. They win the benefits today of decisions that may cost the young dearly throughout our days.

All this eats at our mental and emotional health. Tackling people's symptoms with therapy or drugs isn't enough. As Eleanor Robertson argues, our generation 'didn't go crazy in a vacuum'. She's right that treating the results while ignoring the causes is a short-term solution at best.[1]

THE MILLENNIUM BLUES

A couple of years ago the ABS ran the first comprehensive Australian health survey, looking at both the physical and mental health of people across different life stages. The survey found over 37 per cent of people under 24, and almost 30 per cent of people between 25 and 34, are white-knuckling through their days in moderate to extreme psychological distress.[2] The Department of Health reckons the prevalence of mental health issues like depression and anxiety may be up to three times higher among young Australians than across the community as a whole.[3] In a survey by The Australia Institute, younger people were also more likely to report feeling lonely than any other age group, with women in their late teens and 20s experiencing particularly high levels of not-so-splendid isolation.[4]

It's hard to know how my misery-guts generation measures up against the young in the past. Older data on mental health is hard to come by; even if we had it, this wouldn't necessarily paint an accurate picture of people's wellbeing compared with now. Both our understanding of mental health and our willingness to go public about private aches have changed dramatically in the past 20 years. But what little evidence there is suggests mental health has withered for people my age since the late 1990s. In two national surveys of mental health and wellbeing conducted a decade apart, the incidence of anxiety, depression and substance abuse disorders among people aged 25 to 34 increased by more than in any other age group. The proportion of younger people dealing with these problems jumped from one in five to almost one in four. By contrast, the proportion of people over 55 struggling with their mental health held steady across the decade at less than 15 per cent.[5]

So while we can't say for sure that things have got worse on the wellbeing front, today's young Australians certainly aren't tracking well. And why *wouldn't* my generation be sadder than our olds were at the same age? By 30 my parents had a house that wasn't crushing them with debt, three kids, a steady income and a small stash of savings. Today, the data shows many Australians are only beginning to acquire these things at the dawning of their fourth decade. It isn't just material comfort that my friends and I are missing out on because of this delay. We're also kicking away the struts that support emotional wellbeing.

UNATTACHED AND ROOTLESS

If there's one thing I've learned since splintering my own family unit, it is this: a long-term relationship is great insulation against gloom and loneliness. It provides valuable padding for the emotional googlies that life inevitably bowls. I was 19 when I met my future husband and 23 when we married – the first of my friends to walk that plank by a wide margin. That meant he was beside me on the day I graduated university, and through many fidgety nights that followed as I worked out what the hell I'd do with my life. He kissed me on the forehead when I decamped for overseas, and gathered me up at the arrivals gate when I came home wiser and braver many months later. He was the stillness at the centre of my chaotic early adulthood – bearing me up, setting me straight, steering me on.

But we were unusual in that. Twenty years ago, almost half of all women married in their early 20s. Today, it's only slightly more than one in four. The proportion of first marriages between 25 and 29 has jumped 10 per cent in that time, while one in five first-timers are getting hitched at the previously spinster age of 30-plus.[6] This decade-long delay in settling down means many Australians now go through their own 20-something trials and triumphs without anyone standing steadfast by their side.

The same goes for having kids. My son's arrival brought infuriating chatter, mess and clutter. There is now chaos where there was once the calm of Sunday sleep-ins and complex conversations. But there's no surer way to feel part of something beyond yourself than taking care of a small being who turns to you as if to the sunlight. From the 1960s to the late 1990s, the vast majority of women became mothers for the first time in their 20s. By 2007, however, one in four women were waiting until their early 30s to have their first child, a significantly higher proportion than were doing so in their early 20s.[7] In my lifetime alone, the number of babies being born to women in their mid-20s has crashed from 135 per 1000 to just 75, while for women in their mid-30s it has jumped from 57 births per 1000 to 111.[8]

To put off having kids is to hold at a distance the deep satisfactions and webbed bonds of connection they bring with them. Don't mistake me: lazy hours in cafés and late nights in clubs are the shit. When my childless 20-something friends gather round with reports from that frontline, I miss it like hell. But no brunch ever made my heart bloom the way my son's funny little face does when he peeks around the bedroom door first thing in the morning.

Then there's connection to community, a sense of place and belonging. Since marrying in the early '80s, my parents have lived in exactly three places. There's the house they built as a new couple, and the home they upgraded to ahead of our teens. A few years ago they made one further shift, to an age-in-place abode they intend to inhabit until death takes one or both. In each place they slowly spread out roots: joining the Neighbourhood Watch, minding other families' pets, petitioning the local government for park upgrades and new footpaths. My dad could probably have told you the first name of every bloke living within a three-block radius of my childhood home. My mum is still friends today with two women she met through our local pre-school.

Like a lot of people my age, I've kept moving too much to sow seeds in any one community. In the 12 years since I left home I've already moved nine times, and I'm nowhere near settled yet. As I pointed out in Chapter 3, today more than half of all Australians are renting into their 30s. With the standard lease offering just 12 months' tenure and the overheated property market seeing homes change hands like swap cards, life as a tenant means constant mobility. That's why I don't know my current neighbours and really can't see the point in having much to do with them. We're like trains going different places that just happen to be travelling side-by-side for a moment. My friends and I have got so used to this atomised, impermanent existence that we rarely think to question its impact on our emotional wellbeing. But it's surely yet another big cause of younger Australians feeling isolated and adrift.

Our parents and those curmudgeonly newspaper columnists believe we're doing all this on purpose. To them, we're being 'adultescent'. We're the 'rejuveniles' who don't want to part with our youth, grow up and take life seriously. Even some our own age have piled on the critiques, like the British writer Clive Martin. In a column for *Vice* (the *Time* magazine of the internet age) he carped:

> It's no longer just teenagers and students who seem to be running away from real life. It's people in their twenties and thirties, too – people who should really know better but don't seem to know how to do much else. Fully grown, semi-functioning adults who are unwilling to surrender those endless nights spent staring at their own harrowed reflections in club-toilet cisterns . . . [9]

I emailed some of my friends asking for their thoughts on this notion of 'kidulthood'. Are we making ourselves sad with dodgy choices that delay a grown-up existence? The vehemence of their responses surprised even me.

'How can I have a baby when we have to rent out the spare room to pay our mortgage?' wrote one. 'My roommates would really love living with a screaming kid who wakes the whole house at 4 a.m.!' hyperventilated another. That same friend wrote at length about her craving to get married and the life she sometimes imagined sharing with her current squeeze. Her missive ended: 'But how can I pick and stick when I don't know where either of us will be working a year from now, or even where we'll be living?'

True to stereotype, few of my male peers were willing to share more than a few lines texted late at night and several beers in. But one reply made my heart hurt with its tone of quiet resignation. In reflecting on the gulf between the father he studied growing up and the man he saw himself to be, he wrote:

> When my dad asked my mum to marry him, he could confidently offer her a future that had all these things in it. Kids and houses and holidays and people around on the weekend. I can't offer anyone the same because I honestly don't know if I'll be able to provide that kind of life. It doesn't seem fair to expect anyone to gamble on me.

This uncertainty, this instability: *this* is what's really stopping many of today's under-30s from acquiring the accoutrements of a grown-up life. Young Australians aren't avoiding picking partners, having kids and putting down roots. Instead, insecure work, shaky wealth and transitory living mean that for too many, these simply aren't options on the menu.

Wellbeing among Australia's young won't improve until we acknowledge that this matters. At the moment, our material and personal circumstances are too often considered separate realms demanding distinct responses.

Acknowledging that it's all mingled together in one hot mess means changing where we start in seeking solutions. Ultimately, we need to return some stability and security to young Australians' lives so that all of us have a better chance to weave strong bonds of connectedness. Importantly too, that means our olds will need to ditch the 'kidult' critiques and start paying more attention to the way their own choices are constraining ours.

PROGRESS STALLED AND PROSPECTS DENIED

Wellbeing is also affected by whether we feel like participants in the conversation about the future, or simply powerless bystanders. Younger Australians are frequently finding ourselves treated more like the latter than the former.

People my age are markedly more progressive than our parents and grandparents when it comes to today's big policy questions. That's not really surprising since it's fairly well known that – in terms of who they vote for, at least – older people are more conservative.[10] I don't doubt the teens of 1970s Australia were more liberal in their thinking on conscription than their parents who'd seen service in the sands of Egypt. In the same way, those parents would have parted ways with their own olds on issues like bank nationalisation and the virtues of a White Australia. Being more progressive when you're young is yet another life cycle effect.

This attitude gap between old and young doesn't matter much when you're deciding on issues with a pretty limited scope and a short time horizon. If the polity gets it wrong today, you can always fix it tomorrow. The problem is that we're at a juncture where the decisions we make now will have consequences that echo for many decades. I believe many older Australians are forming their views on the big issues of today with nothing like that long view in mind. At the same time, there's an age skew in the electorate and it is growing all the time. So we're seeing inward-looking oldies using their greater political weight to block progressive change that would be in the community's broad best interest.

It's not hard to see how this could happen. Of the 15 million plus voters enrolled in 2014, more than one in three were aged 55 or over. Fewer than one in four were under 35. There are currently *1.8 million* more grey-haired electors in Australia than there are youthful voters.[11] Yet ABS figures show that as shares of the population, the number of Australians in these two age brackets is pretty evenly balanced.[12] So why the imbalance in the voting population? The problem lies with enrolment rates. Far too many young Australians are simply opting out of exercising that most fundamental democratic right: voting.

In the lead-up to the 2013 federal election, the Australian Electoral Commission (AEC) estimated that over 493,000 people under 24 were missing from the electoral roll – more than one in three eligible young voters.[13] In the previous federal election, around 1.4 million eligible voters hadn't bothered to get on the roll. The AEC reckons that no less than 70 per cent of them were aged between 18 and 39.[14] Enrolment rates have been gradually falling across the board since the late 1980s, but they've fallen furthest and fastest among the young. This decline is driven, in part, by a feeling that engagement in formal politics is pointless when the system seems incapable of delivering the right outcomes. The depth of that disengagement is revealed by the fact that only four in 10 Australians under 30 believe democracy is preferable to any other kind of government.[15]

This situation creates a piquant paradox. Young people are stepping back from voting because the political process doesn't seem responsive to our concerns and preferences. But in taking that step back, we're reducing our electoral leverage and actually making it easier for politicians to dismiss our views. As The Australia Institute's Richard Denniss puts it: 'They think, well, there's one group I don't have to make happy, why will I waste time and money solving their problems when they've just told me they don't care?'[16] We are dealing ourselves out of the game.

Because there are fewer of us who matter electorally, it's then harder for young Australians to push for progressive change in the areas we want to see it. To bastardise Disraeli only slightly: decisions are driven by those who show up.[17]

Climate change and renewable energy policy are among the best examples of this problem. Opinion polls consistently show a significant gap between young Australians and older ones on both the perceived importance of these issues and how we should tackle them. For instance, the Climate Institute found 63 per cent of under-35s agreed that climate change poses a serious threat to our way of life. Barely more than half of those aged over 54 agreed.[18] There was also a 15-point gap in the percentage of younger and older Australians saying they'd like to see Australia lead the global response to climate change instead of waiting for other countries to act.

Those differing views presumably explain why one in three Australians over 55 supported abolishing our carbon price in 2013, compared with only around one in five people under 35. They also help make sense of the much stronger support for Australia's Renewable Energy Target (RET) among the young. In the Climate Institute's research, almost half of those in the youngest age bracket said it should be increased from its current level. That's quite a contrast with the oldest group, where only slightly more than one in three were willing to back a higher target.

People my age can't afford to be blasé about avoiding environmental harm when we'll be among those sweating it out in Waterworld 2060. Climate experts believe we have only a short and shrinking window in which to slow the pace of harmful change. Given this, it's appalling that

Australia would actually be scaling back our climate mitigation policies instead of ramping them up. But that's what happens when the most politically influential voices aren't those with a long-term stake in the outcome.

Marriage equality is another area where older Australians are throwing their weight around to obstruct progressive change. In research carried out by the Liberal Party's polling firm, Crosby Textor, nine in 10 women under 34 and eight in 10 men in that age bracket backed allowing same-sex couples to marry. Among those aged 55 to 64 support dropped to six in 10, while less than half of those aged over 65 said they were in favour of it.[19] Do you know how rare it is to have nine in 10 Australians agree about anything? Unless the question is 'Should there be free beer at the cricket?', it's almost unheard of to find that level of unanimity. Yet despite the clear preference younger Australians have to see marriage discrimination dismantled, progress on this is in stalemate in the parliament. Again, this is because more of those who will actually vote are opposed to marriage equality. Much as we might wish for MPs who make decisions based entirely on what's right, the career-ending implications of going against the will of those voters also weighs heavily in their thinking.

This inertia has serious consequences. Young gay and lesbian Australians attempt suicide about six times more often than their straight mates.[20] They experience psychological distress, depression and anxiety at around twice the level reported in the wider community. The refusal by government to legislate acceptance at the highest level of our society filters down as a fog of disapproval that smothers too many of our gay and lesbian loved ones.

Then there's the slow erosion of our individual rights in the digital space. In the past few years, the Australian parliament has progressively scaled back personal liberties as it makes laws governing newer technologies. This has included several attempts to filter the internet, which finally succeeded last year with the passage of laws allowing the blocking of access to bitTorrent sites. The parliament also agreed to force telcos and ISPs to store up to two years' worth of data about what each of us gets up to online and through our ever-present smartphones. Where we are, who we're talking to, what sites we visit – all logged away. Half a dozen security and law enforcement agencies are allowed to dip into this information any time they like, without warning us and without a warrant. Academic Angela Daley describes the laws as 'a mass surveillance program which interferes with the privacy of millions of completely law-abiding people in a very intrusive and totally disproportionate way.'[21] The NSW Council of Civil Liberties agreed, called the changes 'a disproportionate invasion of people's privacy for no proven benefit.'[22]

These metadata changes were pitched as necessary to protect us from terrorism, and it seems nervous older Australians mostly agreed. But younger people didn't buy it: in a survey by the Lowy Institute, less than half of those under 29 supported these new laws.[23] We understand that once lost, our individual rights to privacy and due process are likely gone forever – and that's a scary prospect for people who carry out so much of our lives online.

More practically, it's hard to imagine any political party putting forward punitive plans like those in the 2014 Budget if more young Australians were politically engaged. What government would have guts to propose a six-month wait before people under 30 could access Newstart if they knew every one of those affected would turn out and vote? But when the majority of voters are several decades distant from the lived experience of young people, then why not? Policies that take exclusively from the young become a palatable way to shave billions off the balance sheet; all the better if they punish some so-called bludgers on the way through.

These are just a few recent examples where younger and older Australians diverge in their views and preferences on the right response to important issues. There are plenty more. I'm pissed off about the outcome in every one of these cases, but I'm also worried about the broader problem they point to. That is: the interests of the old and the young very often don't line up these days. They want cheaper power bills; we want a habitable planet. They want tax breaks for their third house; we want to be able to afford a first. They want to feel safe in a world that seems increasingly unfamiliar; we want laws and policies to reflect the change we're living through. Unfortunately, young people's voices currently carry less weight when elected representatives are considering big questions like these.

As I'll discuss in the next chapter, political parties and voting reforms have a role to play in bringing young voters back into the electoral fold. But we also need to take it upon ourselves to reverse this slow shuffle out of the formal political system. My generation can't whinge that no one in power is listening if we refuse to use the most reliable tool around for making them pay attention. This is one area where better outcomes are well within our grasp. We *can* be participants instead of bystanders in the conversation about Australia's future direction. But we have to start by getting off our arses.

*

It all seems pretty bleak at this point, doesn't it? Wherever we look, there are clear signs that today's young Australians are falling behind at work, with our wealth and when it comes to wellbeing.

But here's where we break with the gloomy present and lift our gaze to the horizon. Because not one of the problems I've explored in these past few chapters is intractable or inevitable. There *are* solutions that could see us build a fairer future for today's young Australians and those coming after us. We might not fix it all, or all at once. But we must at least make the effort to stop Australia becoming a country divided between the prosperous old and the precarious young.

We *have* to try. So let's now talk about where we start.

CHAPTER SIX

SO NOW WHAT?

I'm pretty sure my friends and I are cooked. The trends I've talked about are bearing down on us in ways we may not ever fully get out from under. We certainly seem set to stand out as a distinct cohort as we travel through the rest of our days. With compressed careers, less wealth, more debt and personal lives delayed, our middle and old age is likely to look very different from the existence our parents and grandparents enjoyed before us.

I'm ropeable about that; about the lost opportunities, the wasted potential, the casual inequity. I feel ripped off that the future that beckoned from my childhood has turned out to be a mirage, always shifting further off into the horizon.

But now what? One of the things that frustrates me most about older generations is their 'I'm all right, Jack' refusal to look beyond their own circumstances. We shouldn't be like them. It may be too late for us in some ways, but there's still plenty we can do to ensure that those coming after us know a fairer future.

There's no single set of solutions to this complicated jumble of economic, social and demographic challenges. There almost never is in public policy. So what follows is a range of practical suggestions. Feel free to argue with them, pick them apart, take their components and turn them into something else. At least then we'll be having a conversation that is now well overdue: about how we get from where we are today to a country of opportunity for old and young alike.

WORK

Improving young people's work prospects demands three things. First, we need better training to get as many Australians as possible into high-skill, good-quality jobs. With more focused training, young people won't be confined to low-wage, casual jobs at the dodgy end of the service sector as too many now are.

Next, we must ensure low-skill jobs in the growth industries of the coming decades are also 'good jobs', offering proper conditions and protections. Wages and conditions for young workers have fallen away, in part, because we as a community have decided to let them do so. We shouldn't repeat this mistake when looking at the low-skill jobs of tomorrow.

Third, we need to support more young people to go

out on their own and build new businesses as an alternative to remaining stuck in the clogged jobs pipeline. This way we won't have to force old people out of good jobs in order to give younger ones the chance to get ahead.

EDUCATION AND TRAINING IS FOR EVERYONE; UNI DOESN'T HAVE TO BE

When we talk about training and high-skill jobs, very often the focus is on funnelling people into university. It is undeniably valuable to increase the number of Australians with degrees – both for our common good and for the individual prospects of coming generations. It is also important to guide students towards degrees that give them skills that are in demand now and will be so in the years ahead. Predicting the future is a game for mugs and swindlers, but I'm willing to bet that science, technology, engineering and maths (STEM) degrees are going to stand tomorrow's students in good stead, come what may.

University matters, but it is only one part of the skills and training story. In 2009 the Australian government announced it wanted to see 40 per cent of people between 25 and 34 holding at least a bachelor degree by 2025. What about the remaining six in 10 young people who'll never enter a lecture hall unless they're there to fix the heating?

It's an uncomfortable truth for some progressives, but university isn't for everyone. Plenty of Australians simply aren't suited to the style of learning on offer there. People like my dad and my brother: good with their hands but fidgety in a classroom. People who like to solve practical problems instead of talking endlessly about theoretical ones. The ones who are bright, canny and curious in a way that has nothing to do with essays, formulas and set readings. We're not doing anywhere near enough to equip *these* young people with the skills they'll need to get good jobs in the years ahead. Refocusing on apprenticeships would be a useful place to start.

In 2014 there were almost 100,000 fewer people undertaking a formal apprenticeship than in 2009 – this despite Australia's population growing by more than 1.5 million people over that period.[1] What's more, only about half of those who start an apprenticeship today will actually see it through to completion – well down on the 75 per cent completion rate for undergraduate degrees.[2]

Apprenticeships are valuable for a number of reasons – the primary one being that they get young people with minimal skills into a workplace where they can earn money while they develop some. Done properly, the combination of on-the-job training and classroom learning supports workers to gain both specialist trade skills and general capabilities like critical thinking and problem solving. A successful apprentice winds up with transferable work experience and recognised qualifications under their tool-belt, greatly improving their chances of securing steady work.

At the moment, Australia is not using the apprenticeship model as well as we could be. What's more, paging through the courses on offer at Australia's TAFEs shows these are still heavily focused on traditional trades like plumbing, carpentry, baking and hairdressing. To attract more young people to apprenticeships and ensure they gain skills for the future, we need to broaden the range and type of training on offer. We're aiming to have more science, technology, engineering and maths students graduate from university, because they can create the 3D printers, medical robots, sensor-enabled traffic grids and other tech goodies that are changing the way we live, work and move around. But these new technologies are also going to create demand for people skilled at installing, maintaining and repairing them. We're going to need mechanics who know how to service a car that has as much on-board computing power as a desk full of iMacs. Electrical engineers who can repair a 3D printer. Communications specialists who are handy at keeping sensor networks humming. And technicians who can fix finely calibrated medical equipment. These are the tradies of the 21st century: less bum crack, more bundled ADSL installation. We need to start skilling them now by boosting STEM *trades* just as much as STEM degrees.

Germany's world-leading apprenticeship system offers a useful template. In that country, apprenticeships are offered in a hugely diverse range of fields – from banking and IT to advanced manufacturing, hospitality and sales, as well as more traditional trades. As a proportion of the workforce, more than twice as many people undertake an apprenticeship as do so in Australia. Furthermore, over 80 per cent of workers who start one actually end up completing it.[3]

German apprentices are paid less than Australian ones,[4] but their employers invest far more in their training and get subsidies from the federal government to do so.[5] Perhaps because of this combination of diversity and quality, doing an apprenticeship is as respectable a career path as any in Germany. It certainly isn't seen as a fallback option for failing kids the way it too often is in Australia.

It's important to note that getting young people into TAFE isn't enough on its own. Doing a certificate IV or diploma doesn't help if it's not connected to skills employers are actually looking for. The beauty of apprenticeships is that they link training and work in a direct way.

ORGANISING A WAY TO TURN BAD JOBS TO GOOD

Jobs based on technology and innovation are the ones everyone wants to talk about. This is work that has the futuristic feel of Isaac Asimov – smart, sterile and safe. If we look at where demography and technology are leading, however, it's likely there's also going to be a new wave of demand for particular types of relatively low-skill work. These jobs could end up being dirty, unreliable and poorly paid, or they could underpin a new working middle class.

Which outcome prevails depends a lot on the steps we take to safeguard rights and protections in these sectors.

For instance, with Australia getting older and more people living into their 80s and beyond, the aged care and health sectors are almost guaranteed to see many more jobs for in-home helpers and medical aides, carers, rehabilitation techs and the like. Physically demanding, emotionally taxing and often mucky and gross, these jobs will inevitably be filled by people who lack more advanced skills.

Unionisation will help see these jobs become quality middle-class ones. The lack of it just about guarantees they will be insecure, poorly paid and unsafe. It is almost impossible to overstate how important collective industrial action by, and on behalf of, workers in sectors like these will be in getting them a good deal. But unions are mass-member organisations. They only work well when a significant segment of the workforce chooses to sign up. As I noted in Chapter 1, union membership has been dropping like a stone for the past 20 years, particularly among the young.

Unions like United Voice offer a good lesson in turning this trend around. A few years back, it decided to have a crack at something that hadn't been done in Australia for a long time: genuine community organising. Its Big Steps and Clean Start initiatives aimed to mobilise union members, non-members and those in the wider community to campaign for better pay and conditions for childcare workers and contract cleaners. These campaigns started with thousands of conversations: childcare workers talking to parents about why their wages make it hard to stay in the industry; cleaners chatting with office workers about their crappy conditions and uncertain hours. These conversations educated the community and gradually mobilised a groundswell of support that put pressure on governments and businesses to act. This pressure was ratcheted up by letter-writing campaigns, media-savvy events (like giving a Golden Toilet Brush Award to the companies that had done least to give workers a fair deal over the past year) and online information-sharing. In this way, United Voice reached well beyond its own membership to engage the wider community in making the case for change, and did so in a low-key, positive way.

This approach has so far proved to be very successful: the cleaners' campaign saw a range of big employers sign on to Clean Start collective agreements that boosted pay and conditions for CBD office workers in 2008, and re-sign these in 2013.[6] The Big Steps campaign culminated in the Australian government establishing a $300 million fund to improve wages for skilled early childhood educators.[7] Buoyed by these wins, United Voice has more recently turned its focus to the hospitality sector, taking on the casualisation and crappy wages I talked about in Chapter 1. In July 2015 the union stopped the national burger chain Grill'd from using WorkChoices-era contracts that dudded its teenage workers out of weekend penalty rates. Legal action, combined with high-visibility online and media campaigning, also forced the company to reinstate the 20-year-old worker who had first raised concern about the contracts.[8] In taking on these fights in new ways, and winning them, United Voice has shown there can be more to modern unionism than scowling men in high-vis vests.

Along with administering CPR to traditional unionism, we also need to think about the new modes of work being created by companies like Uber and Airtasker. These sharing economy services take the casualisation of work to its logical extreme: there are no jobs, only millions of micro-contracts. No longer are we employees; the sharing economy turns everyone into the CEO of their own small business.

When I was a student and a stay-at-home mum, I would have relished the chance to work the hours that suited me and earn money without the pressures of pleasing a single master. But independent contracting is definitely not all upside. There is a growing need to make sure the balance of power isn't tipped entirely towards the billion-dollar companies that provide the platform for this work.

For instance, these services take a fixed cut of every transaction carried out through their platform. They also set the rules about who gets to bid for work, and whether they stay on the network. At the moment, this is all entirely at the companies' discretion: the service fee may be 20 per cent today, but 50 per cent tomorrow. Getting booted from the service might be as simple a matter as complaining about that fee hike. As these services grow in size and number, we need to work out how the (often young) Australians contracting through them can collectively push back against that corporate might.

Better preparing young people to get high-skill jobs and protecting rights and conditions for those who unavoidably wind up in low-skill ones will do much to address the problems I pointed out in Chapter 1. But they're unlikely to solve the pipeline obstacle for young people wanting to move on and up in their careers. For that, we need to look at making it easier and more appealing for young people to start their own businesses.

BUILDING MORE PIPELINES WITH NEW BUSINESSES

I don't think it's a coincidence that in the past decade we've heard about more and more new companies led by young people. Australia's smash-hit software company Atlassian was founded by a couple of guys just out of their undergraduate degrees. Ruslan Kogan was 23 when he started selling cut-price electronics through Kogan.com. Kristina Karlsson was only a year older when she founded the kikki.K stationery business, now close to ubiquitous in Australian shopping malls.

All of these young people looked at the job market laid out ahead of them and decided to forge their own path instead. Rather than toiling away for years under the grey ceiling, they set up new companies and created their own opportunities. Helping more young Australians do what they've done is a valuable way of getting around the blockage created by older people staying in work for longer.

Starting a new business demands several things: a good idea, some thoughtful planning and the gumption to go out on your own. But above all it requires money, and that's where many young people falter. Borrowing from a bank usually means having a major asset to secure a loan against – no house means no credit. Some are fortunate enough to have family and friends willing to bankroll their big plans, but starting a business shouldn't only be an option for the already wealthy.

For small businesses with upfront equipment costs, an income-contingent loan scheme would be a handy way of helping them get off the ground. Starting a café, a blow-dry bar or a plumbing service requires an initial investment in gear, which then pays for itself over time as the business starts bringing in profits. Australia's HECS scheme lets students borrow money upfront for their degrees and pay this back over time through the tax system. In the same way, a government-backed business loan scheme could allow young entrepreneurs to borrow initial capital and pay it back at a rate linked to their business's income. Just as HECS helps kids from all backgrounds go to university, this kind of loan scheme would open up business ownership to a range of people who would otherwise be unable to get finance.

Another kind of business we'd all like to have more of in Australia is tech-based start-ups – the innovative underdogs that blow up to become billion-dollar listed firms. At the point of inception, these businesses are all about growth rather than finding a reliable local customer base. So allowing them to crowdsource their first funding rounds and offering a tax-free window for any company profits in their early years would go a long way to supporting dozens more Australian-based success stories like Atlassian. The Liberal government's Innovation Statement, released in December 2015, leant heavily on tax breaks for big-money investors without properly tackling either of these two more grassroots issues. A cynic might say that's what you get when your PM is a former venture capitalist with an eye for the financier's side of the deal.

Crowdsourced funding takes the small dollar donation approach of Pozible and Kickstarter, and extends it. Many investors buy a small chunk of a start-up firm; together, their contributions add up to enough capital to get the business going and grow it quickly. In New Zealand, start-ups can raise up to NZ$2 million a year this way, while Belgium and the United Kingdom have also legalised this approach in the past few years. At the time of writing, the Liberal government had just announced a draft crowdfunding framework for Australia that was roundly criticised as too complex and too restrictive to be any use to fledgling businesses. It is not clear if or when this framework will become law; the response from start-ups themselves suggests it needs a serious do-over. Why getting a workable crowdfunding scheme going should be more of a challenge in Australia than any of the other countries that have already done so is a bit of a mystery. But it is one of the top things any government could do to help more start-ups take flight.

It is worth pointing out that new businesses don't only create opportunities for the people who start them. Recent research from the OECD across 18 different countries found that companies less than five years old created 42 per cent of all new jobs, despite accounting for just 17 per cent of all employers.[9] In other words, more new businesses means more Australian jobs, which might be filled by the young, the old or anyone in between. So yes, some of these ideas would cost money. And sure, that's not something the Commonwealth currently has a heap of. But investing in people who have the ideas and energy to create new jobs for themselves and others is surely an outlay worth making.

Alongside finance, there's another factor we need to work on to get more young people starting businesses. I don't know if it's a product of our laidback culture, or the way our business sectors are dominated by a handful of big players, but too few Australians even consider going out on their own as entrepreneurs. A 2015 analysis of Australian university leavers found that big, safe, boring organisations topped the list of preferred employers.[10] Graduates were especially keen to work for consulting giants like

KPMG and EY, the big four banks and the public service. The latest update to the University of Melbourne's huge HILDA survey also shows that just under half of all Australian men, and almost 60 per cent of women, say they aren't prepared to take any financial risk at all.[11]

It's more than a little embarrassing that so many Australians would rather push paper at a big bank than be their own bosses because they're scared of the risk involved. Financing schemes and tax incentives won't be enough to see more people starting new businesses unless we also change the culture around entrepreneurship in this country. Specialised websites such as StartupSmart and TV shows like *Shark Tank* are starting to do this, but positive portrayals of local entrepreneurship are nowhere near mainstream. We also need to do better at demonstrating this is something anyone can have a crack at – the handful of business impresarios who have become household names are almost uniformly middle-aged and middle-class. Setting up more pitch competitions, entrepreneurship programs and mentoring meet-ups would help to give young would-be magnates from all backgrounds the sense that starting a business is possible, with risks that are worth the potential rewards.

*

If we can match more young people to high-skill jobs, protect rights for those who end up in low-skill ones, and find ways for ambitious types to sidestep the standard jobs bottleneck, we'll have tackled the first set of problems putting young Australians on the back foot today.

But if we don't? If we let things go on as they are, tipping more and more young people into badly paid, insecure work that offers only crawling career advancement? That'll mean double trouble for Australia in the years ahead because we'll squander our human capital while forcing future generations to lean more heavily on government throughout their days.

Think about it. Where does someone who starts their career working casually at a café wind up if the only training they ever receive is on the job? The likely peak of their progression is becoming a floor manager or staff supervisor. If fortune smiles, they might snag a steady role with a big hotel chain or an RSL club – one of those behemoth pokie-funded enterprises big enough to pay a regular wage. They'll make $50,000, maybe $60,000 a year and rarely save a cent of it because keeping yourself housed, fed and warm costs at least that much these days, especially if you've got kids. If they're not that lucky, they'll spend decades hopping from one semi-permanent job to another, getting dudded on super and sick pay along the way. After 30 years they'll develop crook knees from standing all day, every day – or the boss will decide they're just a bit too slow and cantankerous. And that'll be it; career over. They'll draw the dole until they are old enough to qualify for the pension. Even when they do, they'll live near penury because they have little saved up to supplement it with. That's a sad story of lost potential if it happens to a single person. It's a scandalous waste of human capital if we let it happen on a generational scale.

While all that is going on, Australia is still going to need those skilled technicians and 21st century tradies I talked about a few pages back. So we'll likely end up importing them from overseas, from countries where they don't think it too much trouble to train their young. They'll flourish in ways our own youth can't, with their in-demand skills and meaningful qualifications. We know what kind of ugliness is engendered when those left behind by our economy see others from elsewhere doing well: One Nation and Reclaim Australia are its vanguard.

Those who've currently captured the good jobs will grow steadily older, staying right where they are. No longer hubs of innovation, our corporations and small businesses, our banks and law firms and universities will become the geriatric wards of the professional world. Young people who can't hack pacing in place and those with entrepreneurial drive will go where there *are* opportunities. That means overseas, where they will help build other economies, other communities – instead of ours. They might be back one day, but then why would they return if Australia is stagnating while their adopted homes in Seoul, Tel Aviv or Seattle are thriving?

If nothing changes, Australia will end up exporting our brightest and condemning the rest of our young to lives of struggle and insecurity. That's not a vision for the future; it's a social and economic nightmare.

Changing the way we work will be critical to stop this from becoming a reality. But so too will securing our financial futures by sorting out the hot mess that is home ownership, saving and debt.

WEALTH (AND DEBT)

As prime minister, John Howard said there were public policy issues, and then there were 'barbecue stoppers'. These were the handful of issues that everyday Australians with little or no interest in politics would be talking about as they stood around the backyard grill on a Saturday afternoon. Howard believed that if a government was seen to understand and be acting on those barbecue stoppers, nothing much else about its performance mattered.

Wealth and debt are the barbecue-stopper issues for people my age. More specifically, housing (un)affordability and its impact on our financial futures is something that preoccupies a great many young Australians. Finding ways to bring home ownership back within reach and reduce the housing debt burden is an urgent challenge if we want to stop current and future generations going backwards compared with our parents. It may not be the only answer, though, given the political obstacles to taking action. Developing alternative sources of wealth, better educating young people about finance and pushing back against efforts to load us up with more debt should also be priorities if we are to tackle the problems every sausage-sanga-eater under 30 is talking about.

BRINGING HOME OWNERSHIP BACK WITHIN REACH

Saul Eslake puts it this way: rising house prices are 'causing social harm because they are widening the gap between those who have houses and those who don't'.[12] If we want to put a stop to that harm, there's a number of steps we could take.

There's one big change that almost every serious economist now believes is necessary. Negative gearing and its interaction with the capital gains tax discount means that the price investors will pay for property is completely disconnected from what an ordinary homebuyer can afford. Reforming one – or both – parts of this set-up would go a very long way towards bringing prices back into line with incomes.

People who know this stuff well have come up with a handful of effective approaches. For instance, the McKell Institute's Richard Holden suggests limiting negative gearing to new homes. This would ensure we continue to add new housing stock at a steady clip while easing some of the demand for established homes.[13] Eslake favours matching tax deductions on interest to the value of the capital gains tax discount – meaning investors could claim only half the tax break they currently enjoy.[14] The Grattan Institute's John Daley and Danielle Wood argue for removing the capital gains tax discount altogether so that it becomes harder to make a windfall profit on loss-leading rentals.[15] *Business Spectator* economics editor Callam Pickering proposes changing the rules so that tax breaks can only be claimed against profits from property assets instead of the income from your day job too.[16]

Each of these policy reshuffles would make it less advantageous to pile your money into multiple investment properties. Taking a chunk of investor demand out of the market would do a lot to stop prices driving up and up the way they have over the past decade. Importantly, prices don't have to actually *fall* for housing to become more affordable over time. They just need to stop growing at over three times the rate of wages so that our salaries and savings have a chance to catch up.

Economists and other wonks are fond of saying that good reforms would be easily made if it weren't for politics. That's a little bit like saying I could fly if it weren't for gravity. In the real world, political calculations can't be separated from policy solutions. And that's why, ultimately, we may not see major changes to negative gearing or capital gains tax anytime soon.

In the absence of action to tackle demand, the other way to increase housing affordability is to look at ways to increase supply. More properties to go around will take a bit of the heat out of the bidding war between investors and owner/occupiers. Some analysts suggest that supply isn't really a problem anymore as new housing may catch up with population growth in the next few years. But that overlooks the huge pent-up demand from people who have been priced out of the market. We're going to need to build *a lot* more homes than we currently have before we start approaching a better balance between demand and supply.

Two of the most common ways to increase supply in the past were to release more land for development, and to streamline approvals processes so that developers can get properties built more quickly. The problem with the first of these approaches is that the new land now available for development in our major cities is miles from anywhere most people want to live. The problem with the second is that too often projects get knocked back by local councils protecting the interests of those who already live in an area at the expense of others who might like the same opportunity.

To improve housing supply now, what we really need in Australia's cities is urban infill. That means putting more properties on existing land in the suburbs near where people work, redeveloping old industrial sites and making much better use of dead space along train lines, highways and reserves. That has turned out to be much harder than it should have been over the past few decades, but two changes could help ease the way.

Firstly, levying land tax on all properties – including residential housing – would increase the incentive for landowners to make the most of their patch of earth. Sitting on a huge block in Randwick suddenly looks much less attractive to a retired couple when it comes with a big yearly tax bill. Holding on to a piece of factory wasteland in Collingwood makes little sense when it starts costing more money in tax than it will earn in appreciated value. Levying tax this way creates an incentive for owners to put more properties on their land so the cost can be distributed – or to sell up to someone who will.

Secondly, we should take responsibility for approving new developments in major cities out of the hands of local governments. Letting local councils decide whether developments go ahead has proved to be a recipe for flat-out NIMBY despotism. That's because councils are run by people with a conflict of interest in any decision about growth: those who are from the affected area and have direct connections to the communities that are the most likely to kick up a fuss. What's more, local councils don't have to worry about where a housing project and all its future residents might go if they deny approval – there's always a vague 'somewhere else' to wave them off to.

By contrast, state governments have to think about the interests of *everyone* who lives in their city, not just a handful of cranky neighbours. They have to answer the question of where else residents might go if they can't be housed in a particular spot. And they are better able to withstand self-interested lobbying from a few when their decisions will be of benefit to many.

Victoria's Metropolitan Planning Authority is one example of a body that could manage this kind of responsibility. Established by the Baillieu government in 2013, the authority is charged with looking ahead to future housing and infrastructure needs. It then falls to the state government to fund and deliver those big infrastructure works, and local councils to approve individual housing projects and developments. Giving a body like the Metropolitan Planning Authority the power to *approve* developments as well as plan for them would enable a serious, coordinated approach to unlocking more land for housing supply and increasing urban infill. It would be even better if each major Australian city had a body like this that was statutorily independent from government. This would avoid the temptation for state governments to game development decisions in electorally important seats. Local governments will cry foul at the idea of having their planning powers taken away. But if we want to get housing right in our major cities, the past 20-odd years have proven letting little councils make big development decisions isn't going to get the job done.

None of these changes would make housing more affordable and accessible right away. That's probably a good thing, because there's an awful lot of wealth tied up in Australian property. If prices crashed suddenly, our parents' retirement plans would be royally stuffed. So even if we scrapped negative gearing or changed how land is taxed tomorrow, property prices would ideally come back into balance with incomes over a number of years. In the meantime, then, we need to work on alternative ways for young people to build wealth and manage debt. It's a false dichotomy to think the only financial options are owning a home or having nothing to your name whatsoever – although that's pretty much how most young Australians approach financial planning.

GROW MONEY FOR MO' MONEY

Rich people make use of their money. They buy shares, start businesses, take out bonds. The one thing they don't do is leave it sitting in a savings account earning next to no interest for years at a time.

Starting a business is one way to create wealth, as well as being a good way to get around blockages in the jobs pipeline. I'm not even talking about the funky little companies that unexpectedly go global and end up worth millions – although that's certainly one way to get rich. I'm thinking more about small businesses like my dad's plumbing outfit, slowly and steadily built up over years and decades. His was nothing flashy, just a solid local firm that turned over a modest profit and grew a little more with every passing year. In building that business, Dad set himself up with a source of wealth that had nothing to do with owning property.

Investing in *other people's* businesses is another way the rich get richer. The crowd-sourced equity funding model discussed a few pages back could give young people a useful start in this by allowing us to make small investments and gain equity in emerging companies. These investments don't need to be large – in Belgium, investors are actually prohibited from putting more than €1000 into any one business. Even a small stake can generate returns that provide the seed funding for further investing, starting another business or growing a stash of super. With start-ups, too, there's always the chance that your chosen company becomes the next Facebook and makes you indecently rich.

Then there's more mainstream investing. I'm a little embarrassed to admit it, but I'd never heard of index funds until I went to work for an economist at the age of 28.[17] I didn't know there are ways to grow your money that don't involve doing the fiddly work of picking stocks and monitoring the share market yourself. I was completely ignorant of the potential rewards and manageable risks involved in investing money. Even as a middle class, educated individual, my sole frame of reference for the stock market was the cocaine, tits and pride-before-a-fall tale of Charlie Sheen's character in *Wall Street*.

At the moment, investing tends to be something people come to in late midlife, when they start thinking about how to maximise the hoard they've got set aside for retirement. But there's no reason why younger people can't also get in on the action – with an annual tax return, a 21st birthday windfall or a few thousand dollars in savings.

Our main obstacle is a lack of knowledge about how and where to invest that money well; this can be fixed with better financial education.

The Australian Securities and Investments Commission's MoneySmart Schools program is an example of financial training that can make a difference. It teaches Australian schoolkids practical financial skills like budgeting and saving, basic business management, how markets work and good financial decision-making. Only about 15 per cent of schools took part in the program in the last year, so we need to dramatically increase the uptake if it's going to have a real impact.[18]

The UK's Student Investor Challenge also gives young people hands-on practice at turning a brass razoo into a goldmine. Over 100,000 students from 2500 schools took part in the 2014 challenge, which pitted teams against each other to see who could grow the largest return on a virtual £100,000 investment. The Australian Securities Exchange runs a similar schools trading competition, but uptake is nowhere near as high and tends to be concentrated among rich private schools. The kids at your local public school should have just as much chance to learn these skills as darling Jonty and Octavia at Geelong Grammar.

On the other side of the ledger, improving financial education creates an opportunity to develop better understanding about debt. Why shouldn't you continually roll over credit card debts from month to month? How much mortgage debt can you really afford? Why are company store cards often far more expensive than they seem? These are questions too few young Australians are equipped to answer. What's more, many of the sources we turn to for information about our debts have a deep conflict of interest. Credit card companies, banks and consumer lenders are like that bad-influence friend we all have – the one who insists you should have one more drink instead of admitting your double vision means you've had enough. Better financial education alone is unlikely to end young Australians' credit addiction. But it could lead to some better-informed decisions.

There's no getting around the fact that growing wealth often means laying out some money to begin with – whether for housing, stocks or a new business. But the other side of wealth creation is saving. That's why – dry though the subject is – superannuation should never be left out of any conversation about young Australians and our financial futures.

SUPER SETTINGS FOR BIGGER SAVINGS

Saving for retirement generally sits just below prostate health on the list of things young people can be bothered worrying about. Ironically, though, saving does the most good when you start young because of the magic of compound interest. For this reason, it's incredibly important that we get our superannuation settings right in order to set ourselves up for a secure old age.

The immediate priority is to undo the harms the Coalition government has done to superannuation since taking office. That means bringing back scheduled increases in the super contribution rate. It also means doing something about the tax treatment of super for the lowest-paid Australians, a group that includes a significant majority of young workers.

It only takes a little bit of maths to see why the first of these two initiatives is so important. At the moment, someone earning the median wage sets aside about $133 a week in super. Over a 40-year career with interest rates at their long-run average, they'll retire with super savings of a bit over $800,000.[19] That sounds like a lot, but remember it may have to last 25 years or more. Recall too that many of today's young workers can't afford to buy a house until well into our 30s or 40s – if at all – so we'll need to service a mortgage with those savings on top of paying for our other living costs. By contrast, someone who earns the same wage but puts aside 12 per cent over four decades ends up with a retirement fund worth over $1.1 million. That's a much healthier sum, and about what the super industry's peak body recommends having up your sleeve for a comfortable retirement. Since there was no good rationale given for freezing the super rate in the first place, there's no reason why we shouldn't go back to gradually raising it over the next few years.

At the same time, we really must do something about the way super is taxed. Most of the discussion focuses on the big breaks available to those at the top, which I agree are an unfair boondoggle for already-wealthy Boomers. But it is nothing short of an outrage that the lowest-paid Australians pay 15 per cent more tax on their super contributions than they do on their regular earnings. One of the reasons the low-income super contribution scheme is so valuable is that it makes up for what low-paid workers lose through the inequity of super taxes being levied at a flat rate. We should either bed this down as a permanent part of the tax system, or find some other way to cut the super tax rate for Australians on the lowest incomes. One simple proposal, laid out recently by Baptist Care Australia, is to set the tax on super contributions at half of an individual's marginal tax rate.[20] This would see the lowest-paid Australians pay no tax at all on their contributions; anyone earning up to $80,000 would also get a tax cut. Making super taxes fairer for the poorest Australians isn't a change anyone with an ounce of decency can disagree with. So we should get on with fixing this while the argument rages about reducing tax breaks for the richest.

Once we've tackled these two urgent issues, we should also give thought to how changing the investment settings for super can help young people grow a larger cache for their retirement. At the moment, over 80 per cent of Australians have their super in their provider's default fund, which in most cases is a balanced investment option offering relatively low returns but also little risk.[21] That's a good strategy for older people, but younger

Australians would actually be better off having their super in a higher-risk, higher-growth fund. Again, this is because any early savings translate into a big boost to the total figure you retire with. As younger people are investing over decades, they can also afford to ride out and rebuild after any losses that may result from investing in higher-risk funds. So a system that saw people under 40 automatically allocated to growth funds would be a simple way to increase savings. They could then switch back to balanced funds after 40 to ensure these early gains are protected. Some people are uncomfortable with this kind of 'nudge' policymaking because they see it as paternalistic to guide other people's choices. But as that 80 per cent figure shows, it's a simple fact that most Australians don't consciously choose what happens to their super. Given this, we should do what we can to see it invested well on their behalf.

A FINAL DIATRIBE ABOUT DEBT

In the past few pages I've argued that improving work prospects and incomes, making housing more affordable and increasing financial literacy would all help lighten the debt load on young Australians. These are practical changes, and important ones at that. To properly guard against more straitened financial futures though, we also need to resist persistent attempts to shift public investment off into private debt.

The recent proposal to deregulate university fees is just one example of this. To achieve savings on its books, the Liberal government was prepared to slash public funding for unis and let the debt students would take on for their degrees quintuple. I don't doubt we'll see more proposals like this if Australia's budgetary slump continues and concern about the cost of caring for our aged grows. Health and childcare fees immediately come to mind as other areas where future governments may demand users pay much more so that they can cut back public funding and subsidies. This would be a formula for skyrocketing personal debt.

The bottom line is that things like education, healthcare and early childhood learning are investments. Our governments *should* spend money on these things – not only because it does good for individuals, but also because it benefits our society and economy as a whole. No government should be allowed to get away with pulling back from core responsibilities like these and leaving Australians mired in debt. One positive to emerge from the university fee deregulation kerfuffle was to show that we, as a community, *can* win fights about this. Dedicated opposition and sustained political campaigning effectively killed off that noxious plan. But we must be prepared to keep having these fights as often as necessary in the years ahead to defend proper public investment in services. The alternative will only bring about a more debt-burdened future for each of us.

At the risk of sounding like the worst kind of under-graduate Marxist, wealth is a form of power. If we don't change tack now, if we allow it to become ever-more concentrated in the hands of the aged, this is going to dramatically redraw Australia's social contract.

Take a look at housing. If more and more people can't afford to buy until middle-age or beyond, this makes them reliant on rentals owned by others. That will shift the balance of power in our community in a very tangible way. The landlord class has an upper hand over those who must plead for their shelter; anyone who has recently been through the demoralising experience of rental vetting knows this to be so. Champions of democracy have spent 300 years tearing down systems that saw propertied aristocrats holding power over their tenant serfs, yet increasingly owning property once again gives you the go-ahead to decide how others live, with whom and for how long. Try renting a city apartment with a dog, small kids or an undergraduate share group and then tell me that isn't the case.

Similarly, Australians set great store by the idea that we're all equal. Everyone is a mate; tall poppies get their heads lopped clean off. But how can this collective sense of self be sustained as the ageing rich pull away from the rest? It can't, which is why we're seeing the emergence of a competing national tale; one of 'lifters' and 'leaners'. Virtuous are the lifters in this story – those who pay the bulk of taxes, generate jobs in their businesses and keep cash registers ringing with their enthusiastic spending. Wayward are the leaners – those who draw support from the government, spend more than they save and fall behind in their debts. This notion of lifters and leaners unburdens the well-off from the restraints of egalitarianism. It gives them scope to defend policies and settings that heavily favour them without needing to account for the negative impacts on others. It takes wealth, converts it to power and uses that to bolster the position of those already on top. We're watching this happen right now with the perpetuation of the tax, superannuation and other policies I've explored in the past few chapters.

So if nothing changes with wealth and debt, the problem isn't only that Australia will grow less equal. We will also lose the belief that *being equal matters*; that it is part of who we are and what we stand for as a community. That loss would harm our collective future at least as much as the redistribution of wealth from young to old is harming some of us individually today.

WELLBEING

Making the changes I've canvassed in these pages would do much to make life more stable and secure for young Australians. But what about my generation's emotional malaise?

It has taken a couple of decades for the gaps between young and old to open out as wide as they have. Our opportunities and fortunes have gradually shrunk over many years; none of this happened yesterday. So it's realistic to assume the problems I've been talking about here won't be solved overnight.

That doesn't mean we should resign ourselves to another decade of depression. While we're working away at the big problems, there are a couple of quick steps we could take to make life a little less transitory and a bit more connected. We should also be working urgently on practical ways to influence the political process. None of the changes I've outlined in the past few pages will happen without political pressure, and we'll need to be the ones piling it on.

ROOTING DOWN THE RENTAL LIFE

While I'm not sure if I want to own a house again, I would very much like to feel I have a home. Australia's current rental laws definitely do not lend themselves to that. Quite the opposite – at every turn they underline that you're only taking temporary shelter in someone else's space. For instance, it's rare to find a landlord willing to offer more than a 12-month lease. While you can roll over to a new contract when the old one expires, owners can also take this opportunity to hike the rent or boot you out because they'd prefer a different type of tenant. In states like Victoria, tenants can also be made to vacate if their landlord wants to sell, as empty properties are more appealing than ones with pesky residents in place. There's also the fact that everything from hanging a picture to painting a wall requires approval from your propertied overlord, which isn't exactly conducive to making your rented house feel like a home. After my most recent property inspection, I received a note from the estate agent chiding me for sticking up some of my son's drawings on the kitchen walls. The agent officiously pointed out that using sticky-tape on the precious painted surfaces could be reason enough to take some of my bond.

Since more and more Australians are now renting for longer, it is worth pursuing tenancy laws that encourage long-term residency. Turning again to Germany, that country's approach proves it is possible to have stable housing without needing to own it. Leases are often open-ended rather than fixed-term. This fosters an assumption that tenants will stick around for years and make the place their own. Then there are strict rules governing when tenants can be asked to vacate, with notice periods stretching up to six months when someone has been resident for more than five years.[22] Germany has long had laws capping rent increases to 20 per cent over three years; more recently, Berlin has moved to rein in rents further by setting an average price per square metre for each district and banning landlords from charging more than 10 per cent above this.[23] Because tenants are in for the long haul, rights around what you can do with the place also skew in their favour – planting a garden or painting a wall aren't the hanging offences some Australian landlords treat them as.

Together, all these pro-tenant rules make it far more feasible and desirable to rent in one place for a long time. As journalist Feargus O'Sullivan puts it, Germany's approach is built on the belief that 'housing is an essential public resource first, a speculative good second'.[24] Australia's current rules embody exactly the opposite view: if you can't afford your own house, shut up and take whatever bone those who can are willing to throw you.

Renting in one place for the long-term doesn't just make life more stable and settled. It also allows one to put down roots in a community and build the connections that help us feel less alone. Since we've fallen out of the habit of social connectedness though, these networks aren't likely to grow as naturally and effortlessly as they did in my parents' day. That's why the recent emergence of apps and online social networks that foster local connectedness is a positive development we should get behind.

Nabo is one new suburb-based social network that rolled out across Australia in 2015. Instead of linking up people who already know one another, the platform connects strangers who live in the same area by letting them know about local events and community initiatives. The idea is that you join up with people online to get involved in activities in your patch of the world. Because the network limits contacts to people in your suburb, it offers an online version of the school-gate and corner-shop conversations that were once the basis for getting to know your neighbours. In the United States, a similar service called NextDoor launched in 2011 and is now operating in over 77,000 neighbourhoods. It has been particularly successful in drawing communities together to tackle shared problems like petty crime, as well as building up facilities like community gardens and playgrounds.

Changing rental laws and backing neighbourhood social networks are two small things we could do right now to tackle the rootlessness that eats at young people's wellbeing. Equally important is to get young Australians off the sidelines of national politics and into the places where decisions get made.

TAKING BACK OUR VOICE

There's one often-scoffed-at electoral reform that would do much to overcome apathy and draw young people back into the electoral system: letting them vote at 16. That's not because these teens are more conscientious or politically involved than their 18-year-old counterparts – far from it. It's simply that the practical hurdles of getting someone to a ballot box are more easily overcome at 16 than a couple of years later.

First, 16-year-olds are almost all at school. So encouraging them to enrol is as simple as handing out the forms at an assembly or while taking morning attendance. At 18, potential voters have already started to disperse into uni, work and elsewhere, which makes getting enrolment information to them and ensuring they complete it a far bigger ask. Second, when someone enrols at 16 the address that goes on the form is most likely to be their parents' home. That's usually a much more permanent address than whatever share house or dorm they're dossing down in during their first year out of home. One of the main reasons people fall off the electoral roll is because they don't update their details as they move from place to place. So being enrolled at the family home makes it easier to keep track of your enrolment and stay registered. Finally, because 16-year-old voters would generally be living at home on their first election day, their parents would mostly likely chivvy them along to cast a ballot. Research from countries with non-compulsory voting tells us that having someone in a house who votes makes it more likely that their housemates will too; social pressure works for voting just as much as for teen smoking and shagging.[25] So instead of being in an environment where *no one* may be enrolled or voting – as 18-year-old Australians now too often are – they would be surrounded by those who can nudge them towards turning out for that first vote.

All this matters because voting is habit-forming.[26] Miss your first election and you're much less likely to vote in the next one. Skip a couple in a row and the chances of coming back to the ballot box in the future become very slim indeed. So getting young people to turn up at their first eligible election is crucial for instilling the regular habit of voting.

Aside from hooking them at the first opportunity, giving 16-year-olds the right to vote would, on current figures, add more than half a million more voters to the mix.[27] As I mentioned in Chapter 5, the electorate currently skews old because of non-enrolment by the young. But in the future it will also do so because Australia as a whole will have more older people than young ones. Bringing in more young voters by lowering the voting age won't entirely cancel this out, but it will help to even off the demographics a bit.

With a more balanced electorate, it would be harder for older Australians to stymie change on issues like climate change or marriage equality. Politicians would also be far more cautious about proposing punitive policies that hit the young, like the Coalition's plan to impose a six-month waiting period for Newstart. I'm not suggesting we need a youthful majority to overpower the old; this is not an argument for replacing a gerontocracy with a dictatorship of the baby-faced. But if the electorate was more balanced across the ages, we'd then be able to have real debates about these big issues without young *or* old having an automatic upper hand.

If we're uncomfortable with the idea of letting hormonal and half-formed humans vote, an alternative would be to ban people over a certain age from voting to ensure a fairly balanced electorate. Someone who is 85 or 90 has very little stake in political and policy decisions, because their odds of living to see them through are fairly low. These ancients are also the opposite of those rebelling American colonials: they get representation without making any ongoing contribution in taxation. Please note this isn't a serious proposal: voting is a fundamental right that shouldn't be stripped away so blithely. But the demographic imbalance in the electorate *is* going to get worse unless we find ways to counteract it. Letting people vote two years earlier seems like an easy (partial) fix.

Of course, voting isn't the only way to influence national decision-making. Another way to give young people more of a voice in the conversations that affect our common future is to ensure they have the skills and knowledge to take part. Loath though I am to suggest adding one more thing to the crowded Australian curriculum, quality civics education in schools would help. I don't mean 1950s-style rote learning of the words to the national anthem. I mean a serious introduction to the channels of change. How to write to an MP in a way that provokes a thoughtful, original response. How to lay out a policy argument that can change minds. How to participate in public inquiries, comment on draft legislation, mobilise an effective community campaign (believe me, there's more to it than a Facebook petition). I've seen how this changes outcomes. If you don't believe that it does, think on this: big businesses, unions and lobby groups do it all. They do it because they know that being part of the conversation is the best way to influence what gets decided at the end of it. Helping young Australians develop the skills and know-how to do this too would help to cure our democratic discontents.

Finally, for better or for worse, our political system is structured around formal parties. Independents and micro-movements are on the rise, for sure, but political parties are going to be the vehicle for effecting real political change for a long time yet. So young people need to get involved with parties just as much as they do with policy and governmental processes. To help hook them in, Australia's major political parties will need to recognise and adapt to the ways political engagement has changed in the past few decades.

For my money, the most important change has been the shift from location-based to issues-based involvement. Twenty or 30 years ago, being involved in politics meant joining the local branch of your preferred party, where you'd be in good company with your neighbours and other acquaintances who lived in your area. Political activism focused on issues that were broadly location-based: funding and services for local schools, the quality of the hospital down the road. There'd be some discussion of wider issues and probably a handful of members with bigger agendas – they'd be the ones sent off to represent the branch in state and national forums. But the locus was the suburb and neighbourhood, with parties building from, and reinforcing, existing ties to a particular place.

Barring a few tweaks and rule changes, that's basically still how both the Labor and Liberal parties are set up.

However, this structure doesn't fit with the lives of today's young Australians. Because we are far more mobile, and often disconnected from the communities we live in, going to a branch meeting organised by geography can mean sitting in a room of strangers. Not only that, but with little connection to any one place, we also may have no real reason to care about what goes on locally. Instead, we engage with politics through the prism of our passions and interests. This means focusing on things that may be happening on the other side of the country or at the other end of the world. That's why restructuring around issues could help make political parties more appealing to the young. Within Labor, for example, groups have sprung up in the past few years bringing together people who care about everything from the environment to LGBTI issues, refugees and innovation. Participation in these groups is currently treated as an optional add-on – to be properly 'active' still means grinding through tedious local branch meetings that make self-immolation seem like a fun night out. But restructuring to make these issue-based groups the centre of activity would better align parties with the kind of involvement younger people are yelling out for. It would also bring political parties into closer and more collegial contact with outside groups like NGOs, grassroots campaigns and activists – creating a pathway for fellow travellers to become active members and strengthening links in the community.

Oh, and if we bend over backwards like this to create an electoral system in which young Australians can be active, and the bastards *still* fail to turn up? Then bring on the fines. Far bigger ones than the $20 excuse for a penalty that is handed out today. This country's future is too important to be decided exclusively by the grey crowd who let things get so bad in the first place.

Since 1984, our national anthem has opened with the words: 'Australians all let us rejoice, for we are young and free.' Once a proud declaration of our independence from the Old World, these words will take on an increasingly bitter ring in years to come if we do not help young people find a voice and influence the big debates that so affect our futures. Young and free – to do what? Change what? Decide what? If things go on as they are, Australia will become a gerontocracy where only the views of the aged count and progress falls well behind preserving present advantage as the number-one political priority. Instead of acting on climate change and the other pressing issues of today, we'll put this off until some crisis forces a future government's hand. At that point, the costs and impacts will be far greater and the polity will yelp: why didn't we act sooner?

The answer will be: because there was no one left to strain against the inertia of the status quo. Young people will long since have given up trying to make our voices heard through formal channels, preferring instead to gather in protest groups on the sidelines or withdraw from politics altogether. The battle of ideas, the clash of perspectives and wants and needs that drives change forward will have been replaced by a uniform group of grey heads nodding in furious agreement that things are just fine as they are.

Quite simply, Australia will lose the ability to adapt and rise to the challenges of our times if there is no one left in the room crying 'revolution!' in the face of the status quo. That's why re-engaging young people in national politics isn't only important for improving our wellbeing; it is also critical for protecting Australian politics itself from succumbing to a dangerous stasis.

*

Here's what I want for the coming generations.

Skills that give them options and security. Representation that protects their rights. Opportunities and the capacity to chase them. I want them to know some financial stability, and own a fair share of this country's prosperity. Above all, I want them to build lives with meaning from those foundations; to feel steady, secure, whole.

In the first five chapters I explored where the gaps are opening up between Australia's young and our old. The ideas I've just laid out aim to improve young people's prospects in work, wealth and wellbeing so that we can get these gaps closing again. Unless we shrink the current levels of intergenerational inequality, tomorrow's young will be no better off than today's. They may even face lives that are further diminished as the trends I've talked about gather pace.

Many of the changes I've outlined in these past few pages are obvious and urgent. I'm certainly not the first to call for some of them. But consider this one blueprint for a fairer future. The next step will be to take up our tools and start building it.

CONCLUSION

In May 2015 current Secretary of the Department of Prime Minister and Cabinet Martin Parkinson got to his feet to deliver the graduating address at the University of Adelaide. Born in the late 1950s, educated at several of Australia's best universities, a 20-year veteran of the Australian public service – establishment figures don't come much more established than Martin Parkinson.

This is what he told the bright, accomplished young men and women who sat before him on the cusp of their adult lives:

> My generation has failed you ... despite having benefited from massive growth in living standards, income and wealth. We rode the benefits of others' reform efforts, and thought that success was our doing. In the process, we conflated self-interest with national interest. We lost sight of the big picture and applauded

> the things that made me better off, irrespective of the
> cost to others in our community, or to future
> generations . . . your generation is at risk of being the
> first in modern history whose living standards will be
> lower than those of their parents . . . And the longer
> we wait to address today's challenges . . . the greater
> the damage wilfully being done to future living
> standards.[1]

I don't think a more honest set of sentences has been spoken by an Australian public figure in at least a decade.

Parkinson was prepared to face up to something we all need now to admit: things can't go on as they are. Young Australians are being battered by demographic, technological and economic headwinds that will only gather strength in the years ahead. As I've shown throughout these pages, our current national settings provide little in the way of shelter. Often, in fact, they make those headwinds worse.

We are seeing the development of a lopsided Australia where young and old live differently. Good jobs, comfortable wealth and the wellbeing that comes with both are increasingly being concentrated in the arthritic hands of older people. Meanwhile, younger Australians are forced to live with less: crappier work, lower wealth and worse wellbeing.

This inequality is already a reality for my generation. I can't stress enough that we carry the weight of it heavily.

We experience the unfairness daily in the gap between our means and the milestones of traditional adulthood. We sense it in the divergence between our aspirations and the opportunities in front of us.

We feel like latecomers to some great national feast, where the glutted guests who arrived earlier won't share even the dregs of their wine. If we don't do something about the problems I've laid out here, those coming after us will know deeper inequity still.

I said in the introduction that a more equal future would be one where young Australians enjoy the same opportunities to build stable, secure lives as our parents and grandparents had. That's not so big an ask. But given the circumstances, it will take some big changes to achieve. Young and old Australians alike must have a hand in bringing about those changes.

To the older generations: we know you didn't do all this intentionally or with malice. We don't hold you specifically responsible for creating the problems we're now facing. You just grabbed with both hands the opportunities that appeared in front of you; you've had timing and plenty of luck on your side. But as the damaging impact of current trends and policies on younger Australians becomes increasingly clear, we *will* hold you accountable for what comes next.

If you obstruct the changes that need to happen, knowing what you now know, you are making a deliberate choice to prolong your advantage at the expense of other people. To do nothing is almost as bad – it means looking the other way while inequality rises around you. So choose your next move thoughtfully.

To my friends and peers, as well as those coming after: frankly, we shouldn't rely on them. It's very likely we'll have to design, fight for and deliver those big changes ourselves. Mum and Dad won't be sweeping in to sort things out and kiss it better this time.

Our default positions are cynicism and snark, but being a jaded smartarse never fixed anything. Neither did disengagement and despair. Believe me, I well understand the temptation to throw your hands up and say things are stuffed beyond repair. I've felt that tug of fatalism myself. We've got every right to be angry, frustrated and disappointed. But not one thing will change until we channel those burning, bitter gut reactions into tangible acts.

If we're going to build a fairer future for ourselves and coming generations, we need to get involved. That starts with believing it's possible to bring about change through the institutions we have in front of us. Contrary to what you often hear, they aren't broken. They're just run by people who have good incentives to put other people's interests ahead of ours.

So join a political party. Go to a hearing. Make a submission. Show up. Above all, let go of the idea that there is something lame about caring too much. What's truly feeble is whinging without being willing to act. Change only gets made when we take responsibility for making it.

There is no one path to a more equal future for young and old Australians. I believe in the solutions I've laid out in this book, but won't for a second claim they're the only ones going. We should welcome any ideas that can shrink the intergenerational gap – whether they come from friends, foes or fields unexpected. We must keep trying new things – and failing, and trying again – until the gaps I've pointed out in these pages start closing.

Tackling inequality of any kind isn't easy. There'll be spats and tantrums on the way as those who've conflated self-interest with national interest are obliged to recognise the difference once more. But we'd be failing future generations just as much as those in the past failed us if we decided it is all too hard. So as that former US president with great hair and a penchant for movie-star blondes once said: let us begin.

ACKNOWLEDGMENTS

I have had the good fortune to receive advice, feedback, ideas and support from a number of exceptional people in the course of writing this book, including: Andrew Leigh, Nick Terrell, Thomas McMahon, Tim Watts, Michael Cooney, Danielle Wood, Christine Butterfield, Clare Butterfield, Gareth Hutchens, Matthew Tyler, Nicholas Reece, Hugh Hartigan and Jim Chalmers. I am grateful to every one of you for finding the time and generosity of spirit to offer your thoughts.

I would particularly like to thank Sebastian Zwalf for the road trip that planted the seeds this book grew into; and Sam Dastyari for offering sledging and encouragement in (almost) equal measures.

Thank you to all of my friends and peers who contributed to this book directly and indirectly by sharing your frustrations, fears and hopes for the future. I only hope I have done justice to your stories.

To Chris Feik, Jo Rosenberg and the rest of the Black

Inc. team: thank you firstly for taking a punt on this book, and then for doing so much to try and make that punt pay off. I am honoured and grateful to have worked with you all.

Finally, thank you to the men and women of the Australian Labor Party for the opportunities you have given me, and for continuing to work towards a better future for all Australians – every day.

NOTES

Introduction

1. Chris Richardson, as quoted in Jacob Greber, 'Expert Call on Budget Fix: Target Super', *Australian Financial Review*, 18 February 2015.

2. The Treasury, *2015 Intergenerational Report: Australia in 2050*, Canberra, 2015, pp. 1–14.

3. Productivity Commission, 2013, *An Ageing Australia: Preparing for the Future*, Productivity Commission research paper, Canberra, pp. 10–11.

4. Joe Hockey, interview with Leigh Sales, *7:30*, ABC TV, 5 March 2015.

5. For a further discussion of why popular terms such as 'Baby Boomer' or 'Generation X' describe problematic concepts, see for example: Frank Giancola, 2006, 'The Generation Gap: More Myth Than Reality', *Human Resource Planning*, Vol. 29, No. 4, pp. 32–37; John Quiggin, 'The End of the Generation Game', *Australian Financial Review*, 27 October 2000.

6. John Quiggin (see note 5, this chapter).

7. Nassim Nicholas Taleb, 2010, *The Black Swan: The Impact of the Highly Improbable*, second edition, Random House, New York.

CHAPTER 1. WORK (GETTING IN)

1. David Uren, 'Hardest Time in Decades to Get Work', *Australian*, 7 August 2015.

2. Australian Bureau of Statistics, 2015, *6291.0.55.001 Labour Force, Australia, Detailed*, Table 1: 'Labour Force Status by Social Marital Status, Age and Sex', Canberra.

3. Brotherhood of St Lawrence, 2014, *Australian Youth Unemployment 2014: Snapshot*, Melbourne, pp. 4–5.

4. See, for example, Clive Altshuler, 2013, 'Measurement Problems with Youth Unemployment in the European Union' in *World Economic Situation and Prospects: Weekly Highlights*, Geneva; Steven Hill, 'Youth Unemployment is Overstated', Social Europe, 25 July 2012; John Philpott, 2011, *Getting the Measure of Youth Unemployment*, CIPD, London.

5. Author's own analysis, based on: Australian Bureau of Statistics, 2015, *6202.2 Labour Force, Australia*, Table 22: 'Labour Underutilisation by Age and Sex', Canberra.

6. David Dooley, Joann Prause, Kathleen A. Ham-Rowbottom. 2000, 'Underemployment and Depression: Longitudinal Relationships', *Journal of Health and Social Behaviour*, Vol. 41, No. 4, pp. 421–436.

7. There has also been some growth in casual work in the 65+ workforce, as people retire in better health and seek ways to supplement their retirement income. See: Australian Bureau of Statistics, 2013, *6105.0 Australian Labour Market Statistics*, Table 1: 'Employment Type: Employed Persons by Sex, Full-time/Part-time and Age, August 1992–August 2007 and November 2008–November 2012', Canberra.

8. Author's own analysis, based on: Australian Bureau of Statistics, 2013 (see note 7, this chapter).

9. Australian Council of Trade Unions, 2012, *Lives on Hold: Report of the Independent Inquiry into Insecure Work in Australia*, Melbourne, p. 16.

10. Andrew Leigh, 'Fair Gone? How Governments Can Guard Against Growing Inequality', speech, Australia New Zealand

School of Government VPSC Lecture Series, Melbourne, 19 February 2015.

11. Author's own analysis, based on: Australian Bureau of Statistics, 2014, *63100TS0002 Employee Earnings, Benefits and Trade Union Membership, Australia – Mean Weekly Earnings in Main Job*, Table 4: 'Employees in Main Job, Mean Weekly Earnings in Main Job, by Full-time or Part-time Status in Main Job, by Age Group (Years), by Sex, 1990–2013', Canberra.

12. Australian Bureau of Statistics, 2014 (see note 11, this chapter).

13. See, for example: Bruce Western and Jake Rosenfeld, 2011, 'Unions, Norms and the Rise in American Wage Inequality', *American Sociological Review*, Vol. 76, No. 4, pp. 513–537; Axel Dreher and Noel Gaston, 2006, *Has Globalization Increased Inequality?*, Working Paper No. 140, Eidgenossische Technische Hochschule, Zurich; Maarten Goos and Allen Manning, 2003, *Lousy and Lovely Jobs: The Rising Polarization of Work in Britain*, Centre for Economic Performance, London School of Economics and Politics Science, London.

14. OECD, 2014, *Annual Labour Force Statistics*, Employment by Activities and Status, Paris.

15. Carl Benedikt Frey and Michael A. Osborne, 2013, *The Future of Employment: How Susceptible Are Jobs to Computerisation?*, Working Paper, Oxford Martin School Programme on the Impacts of Future Technology, University of Oxford, Oxford.

16. Australian Bureau of Statistics, 2015, *6291.0.55.003 Labour Force, Australia, Detailed, Quarterly*. Table 04: 'Employed Persons by Industry – Trend, Seasonally Adjusted, Original' Canberra.

17. Australian Bureau of Statistics, 2013, *63100DO023_201308 Employee Earnings, Benefits and Trade Union Membership, Australia*, Table 23: 'Employees (excluding OMIEs) in Main Job, Industry of Main Job – by Whether Had Paid Leave Entitlements in Main Job and Sex – By Trade Union Membership in Main Job', Canberra.

18. Australian Bureau of Statistics, 2014, *5260.0.55.002 Estimates of Industry Multifactor Productivity, Australia*, Table 6: 'Labour Productivity Indexes', Canberra.

19. Jeff Borland, 2014, *Labour Market Snapshot #7*, Department of Economics, University of Melbourne, Melbourne.

20. Jake Rosenfeld, as quoted in Nicholas Kristof, 'The Cost of a Decline in Unions', *New York Times*, 19 February 2015.

21. Australian Bureau of Statistics, 2013, *63100DO023_201308 Employee Earnings, Benefits and Trade Union Membership, Australia*, Table 15: 'Employees in Main Job, Mean Weekly Earnings in Main Job – By Selected Characteristics – By Trade Union Membership in Main Job – By Sex', Canberra.

22. Australian Bureau of Statistics (see note 17, this chapter).

23. Author's own analysis, based on: Australian Bureau of Statistics (see note 11, chapter 1).

CHAPTER 2. WORK (GETTING ON)

1. Australian Bureau of Statistics, 2014, *6105.0 Australian Labour Market Statistics*, Table 1: 'Employment Type: Employed Persons by Sex, Full-time/Part-time and Age, August 1992– August 2007 and November 2008–November 2012', Canberra.

2. Ira Wolfe, 'Gray Ceiling Darkens Job Hopes for Millennials', *Huffington Post Business*, 15 September 2012.

3. The Treasury, 2015, *2015 Intergenerational Report: Australia in 2055*, Canberra, p. 141.

4. Author's own analysis, based on public records. The eight major public service departments are: Department of the Prime Minister and Cabinet; Treasury; Department of Finance; Department of Defence; Department of Foreign Affairs and Trade; Department of Social Services; Department of Employment; and Department of Immigration.

5. Author's own analysis based on public records. The firms included in this particular sample are: NAB, Westpac, ANZ, Commonwealth Bank, St. George Bank, Coles, Woolworths, Myer, David Jones, Telstra, Optus, Qantas, Target Australia, Leighton Holdings, Meriton, Cochlear, Lion and BAE Systems Australia. Including different companies gives slightly different results each time but the trend is consistent in each case: CEOs

of major Australian firms are, on average, older now than they were 25 years ago.

6. Author's own analysis based on official parliamentary biographies.

7. Australian Public Service Commission, 2014, *State of the Service Report 2013–2014*, Canberra.

8. Author's own analysis based on: Australian Public Service Statistical Bulletins 2001–2014, Australian Public Service Commission, Canberra.

9. Australian Bureau of Statistics, 2015, *3101.0 Australian Demographic Statistics*, Table 59: 'Estimated Resident Population by Single Year of Age', Canberra.

10. Author's own analysis, based on: Australian Bureau of Statistics (see note 11, chapter 1).

11. Bernard Keane, 'Country for Old Men: Little Diversity in Abbott's Picks', *Crikey*, 3 March 2014.

12. Kirstie Clements, 'The Age of Entitlement', *Sun-Herald*, 29 March 2015.

13. Australian Bureau of Statistics, 2013, *62090DO007_201302 Labour Mobility, Australia, February 2013*, Table 7: 'Persons Who Worked at Some Time During the Year Ending February 2013, Changes in Employer/Business or Work – by Selected Personal Characteristics', Canberra.

14. Australian Bureau of Statistics, 1994, *6209.0 Labour Mobility, Australia, During the Year Ending February 2014*, Table 4: 'Persons Who Worked at Some Time During the Year Ending February 1994: Summary of Characteristics and Job Mobility', Canberra.

15. Bureau of Labor Statistics, 1997, *Employee Tenure in the Mid-1990s*, Washington.

16. McCrindle Research, 'Job Mobility in Australia', blog, 18 June 2014.

17. John Bret Becton, Harvell Jack Walker and Allison Jones-Farmer, 2014, 'Generational Differences in Workplace Behavior', *Journal of Applied Social Psychology*, Vol. 44, pp. 175–189.

18. Emma Parry and Peter Urwin, 2011, 'Generational Differences in Work Values: A Review of Theory and Evidence', *International Journal of Management Reviews*, Vol. 13, pp. 79–96. They also point out that very few studies on worker attitudes and beliefs go to the effort of teasing out life cycle versus cohort effects. This means that even when these studies do identify distinctions between people at different ages, it's hard to know if these are, in fact, specific to the current crop of youngsters.

19. Ryan Heath, *Please Just F* Off, It's Our Turn Now: Holding Baby Boomers to Account*, Pluto Press, Melbourne, 2004.

CHAPTER 3. WEALTH

1. Australian Bureau of Statistics, 2013, *65540DO001_201112 Household Wealth and Wealth Distribution, Australia, 2011–12*, Table 25: 'Age of Reference Person, Household Characteristics', Canberra.

2. Bernard Salt, as quoted in Alex May, 'Housing Affordability: A Real Problem, or Just a Whinge?', *Sydney Morning Herald*, 29 August 2007.

3. Author's own analysis, based on: Australian Bureau of Statistics, 2013, *65540DO001_201112 Household Wealth and Wealth Distribution*, Australia, 2011–12, Table 24: 'Age of Reference Person, Household Assets and Liabilities', Canberra; Australian Bureau of Statistics, 2005, *6523.0 Household Wealth and Wealth Distribution, Australia, 2003–04*, Table 20: 'Age of Reference Person, Household Assets and Liabilities', Canberra.

4. Author's own analysis, based on: Australian Bureau of Statistics, 2013; 2005 (see note 3, this chapter).

5. John Daley and Danielle Wood, 2014, *The Wealth of Generations*, Grattan Institute Report No. 2014–13, Grattan Institute, Melbourne, pp. 14–15.

6. Australian Bureau of Statistics, 2004, *6523.0.55.001 Household Income and Income Distribution, Australia, 2001–2002*, Table 9A: 'Age of Reference Person', Canberra.

7. Australian Bureau of Statistics, 2013, *65540DO001_201112 Household Wealth and Wealth Distribution, Australia, 2011–2012*, Table 25: 'Age of Reference Person, Household Characteristics', Canberra.

8. Reserve Bank of Australia, 2003, 'Submission to the Productivity Commission First Home Buyer Inquiry', Sydney.

9. Australian Property Monitors, 2012, *March Quarterly Capital City Prices Report*, Sydney; Australian Bureau of Statistics, 2013, *6523.0 Household Income and Income Distribution, Australia, Government Benefits, Taxes and Household Income, Detailed Tables 2011–2012*, Table 11: 'Age of Reference Person, Income, Benefits and Taxes', Canberra.

10. Andrew Haylen, 2014, *House Prices, Ownership and Affordability: Trends in New South Wales*, NSW Parliament Briefing Paper No. 01/2014, Sydney.

11. Saul Eslake, '50 Years of Housing Failure', speech, 122nd Annual Henry George Commemorative Dinner, 2 September 2013, Melbourne.

12. Saul Eslake, 2013 (see note 11, this chapter).

13. Housing Industry Association, 2014, *Housing Australia's Future: Demographic Analysis of Australia's Housing Requirements*, Canberra.

14. Australian Bureau of Statistics, 2015, *8731.0 Building Approvals, Australia*, Table 6: 'Number of Dwelling Units Approved, by Sector, All Series – Australia', Canberra.

15. Australian Taxation Office, 2015, *Taxation Statistics 2012–13 – Individuals*, Table 1: 'Selected Items for Income Years 1978–79 to 2012–13', Canberra.

16. The capital gains tax discount applies to all types of assets, not just property. However, it is not generally considered to have lead to the same negative externalities when applied to assets like shares as it has with housing.

17. Australian Bureau of Statistics, 2013, *65540DO001_201112 Household Wealth and Wealth Distribution, Australia, 2011–12*, Table 24: 'Age of Reference Person, Household Assets and Liabilities', Canberra.

18. For a detailed discussion of the impacts of negative gearing in Australia and a comparison of our scheme with others internationally, see: Jim O'Donnell, 2005, 'Quarantining Interest Deductions for Negatively Geared Rental Property Investments', *e-Journal of Tax Research*, Vol. 3, No.1, pp. 63–113.

19. Reserve Bank of Australia, 2003 (see note 8, chapter 3), p. 3.

20. Michael Pascoe, 'The Great First Home Buyer Myth', *Sydney Morning Herald*, 24 February 2015.

21. Australian Bureau of Statistics, *6523.0.55.001 Household Income and Income Distribution, Australia, 2001–2002*, 2004, Table 9A: 'Age of Reference Person', Canberra; Australian Bureau of Statistics, 2009, 6523.0 *Household Income and Income Distribution, Australia – Detailed Tables, 2007–08*, Table 13A: 'Age of Reference Person,' Canberra; Australian Bureau of Statistics, 2013, *65540DO001_201112 Household Wealth and Wealth Distribution, Australia, 2011–2012*, Table 25: 'Age of Reference Person, Household Characteristics', Canberra.

22. Department of Families and Community Services, 1999, 'Trends in Home Ownership', Canberra.

23. John Daley and Danielle Wood, (see note 5, chapter 3), p. 15.

24. Australian Finance Group, 2015, *Mortgage Index June 2015*, Table 3: 'Average Mortgage Size in Dollars, State by State', Sydney; Australian Bureau of Statistics, 2015, *6302.0 Average Weekly Earnings*, Australia, May 2015, Canberra.

25. Jeff Haden, 'The Only Way to Get Really, Really Rich', *Inc.*, 17 April 2014.

26. Per Davidsson, Paul Steffens and Michael Stuetzer, 2011, *Global Entrepreneurship Monitor: National Entrepreneurial Assessment for Australia*, The Australian Centre for Entrepreneurship Research, Queensland University of Technology, Brisbane, p. 19.

27. Matt Grudnoff, 2015, *A Super Waste of Money: Redesigning Tax Concessions*, policy brief, The Australia Institute, Canberra.

28. Australian Bureau of Statistics, 2013; 2005 (see note 3, chapter 3).

29. Australian National Audit Office, 2015, *Promoting Compliance with Superannuation Guarantee Obligations*, ANAO Report No. 39, 2014–15, Canberra.

30. Eva Cox, 'How Our Super Steals from the Poor to Give to the Rich', *Crikey*, 4 April 2013.

31. Peter Martin, 'Advice for Hockey: Sting Super and Fix the Budget in One Hit', *Sydney Morning Herald*, 16 December 2014.

32. Industry Super Australia, 'Super Changes Will Reduce Australians' Super Nest Eggs', media release, 2 September 2014.

33. Association of Superannuation Funds of Australia. *ASFA Retirement Standard*. March 2015 update. Sydney, 2015

34. Ross Clare, 2014, *Level and Distribution of Retirement Savings*, ASFA Research and Resource Centre, Sydney.

CHAPTER 4. DEBT

1. Foundation for Young Australians, 2014, *Renewing Australia's Promise*, Melbourne, p. 19.

2. Australian Bureau of Statistics, 2014, *4102.0 – Australian Social Trends, 2014. Trends in Household Debt*, Canberra.

3. Australian Bureau of Statistics, 2014 (see note 2, this chapter).

4. Australian Bureau of Statistics, 2013; 2005 (see note 3, chapter 3).

5. Andrew Norton, 2014, *Mapping Australian Higher Education 2014–15*, Grattan Institute, Melbourne, p. 22.

6. Robert Hiltonsmith, 2013, *At What Cost? How Student Debt Reduces Lifetime Wealth*, Demos policy paper, New York.

7. Andrew Beer, as quoted in Matt Wade, 'Higher Student Debts Will Hit Chance of Buying Home', *Sydney Morning Herald*, 17 May 2014.

8. Pauline Chen, 'The Hidden Costs of Medical Student Debt', *The New York Times*, 28 July 2011.

9. National Commission of Audit, 2014, *Towards Responsible Government*, Appendix to the Report of the National Commission of Audit, Vol. 1, Canberra, p. 338.

10. Geoff Sharrock, 'How Much Student Debt Will You Be Facing Post-budget?', *The Conversation*, 15 May 2014, theconversation.com/how-much-student-debt-will-you-be-facing-post-budget-26712.

11. Alan Tapper, Alan Fenna and John Phillimore, 2013, 'Age Bias in the Australian Welfare State', *Agenda*, Vol. 20, No. 1, pp. 1–20.

12. Net benefits are the value of all social transfers after household tax. Examples include pensions, paid parental leave, childcare rebates and income support payments like Newstart.

13. Christopher Pyne, interview with Emma Alberici, *Lateline*, ABC TV, 20 May 2015.

14. Australian Bureau of Statistics, 2013; 2005 (see note 3, chapter 3).

15. Reserve Bank of Australia, 2015, *Household and Business Finances*, Table E7: 'Household Debt – Distribution', Sydney.

16. Martin North, 'Who Pays for What in the Credit Card Business?', *Digital Finance Analytics*, 24 February 2014 (with thanks to John Daley for the tip).

17. Sophie Elsworth, 'Young Adults Drowing in Debt', *Herald Sun*, 14 July 2013.

18. Nicki Dowling, Lauren Hoiles, Tim Corney and David Clark, 'Financial Management and Young Australian Workers', *Youth Studies Australia*, Vol. 27, No. 1., pp. 26–35.

19. Australian Bureau of Statistics, 2015, *5206.0 Australian National Accounts: National Income, Expenditure and Product*, Table 1: 'Key National Accounts Aggregates', Canberra.

CHAPTER 5. WELLBEING

1. Eleanor Robertson, 'Generation Y Didn't Go Crazy in a Vaccum', *Guardian*, 17 October 2014.

2. Australian Bureau of Statistics, 2012, *43640DO004_20112012 Australian Health Survey: First Results, 2011–12 — Australia*, Table 4.1: 'Level of Psychological Distress, Persons', Canberra.

3. Department of Health, 2013, *National Mental Health Report 2013*, Canberra, pp. 90–91.

4. David Baker, 2012, *All the Lonely People: Loneliness in Australia, 2001–2009*, The Australia Institute Research Paper No. 9, Canberra, p. 14.

5. Department of Health, 2013 (see note 3, this chapter).

6. Australian Bureau of Statistics, 2014, *3310.0 Marriages and Divorces, Australia, 2013*, Table 4: 'Females by Age at First Marriage, Remarriage and Total, Selected Years, 1993–2013', Canberra.

7. Alan Hayes, Ruth Weston, Lixia Qu and Matthew Gray, 2010, *Families Then and Now: 1980–2010*, Australian Institute of Family Studies Database, Canberra.

8. Australian Bureau of Statistics, 2014, *3301.0 Births, Australia, 2013*, Table 12.1: 'Age–specific Fertility Rates and Total Fertility Rate, Single Year of Age of Mother – Australia – 1975 to 2013', Canberra.

9. Clive Martin, 'This Sad Generation Doesn't Know When the Party Stops', *Vice*, 1 December 2014.

10. See, for example Achim Goerres, 2008, 'The Grey Vote: Determinants of Older Voters' Party Choice in Britain and West Germany', *Electoral Studies*, Vol. 27, pp. 285–304; James Tilley, 2002, 'Political Generations and Partisanship in the UK, 1964–1997', *Journal of the Royal Statistical Society*, Vol. 165, No. 1, pp. 121–135.

11. Australian Electoral Commission, 2014, *Elector Count by Division, Age Groups and Gender for All States/Territories*, Canberra.

12. Australian Bureau of Statistics, 2014, *31010DO002_201406 Australian Demographic Statistics, June 2014*, Table 6: 'Estimated Resident Population, By Sex and Age Groups – States and Territories – at 30 June 2014', Canberra.

13. Australian Electoral Commission, *AEC Working with Facebook to Encourage Young Voters to Matter in This Election*, media release, 21 June 2013.

14. Australian Electoral Commission spokesperson Phil Diak, interviewed on *AM*, ABC Radio, 17 July 2010.

15. Alex Oliver, 'Are Australians Disenchanted with Democracy?', Lowy Institute Paper delivered as Senate Occasional Lecture, Australian Parliament House, 7 March 2014.

16. Richard Denniss, as quoted in Julia Holman, 'The Youth Don't Care, But They Should', *The Drum*, 17 June 2013.

17. The original quote, from former British prime minister Benjamin Disraeli, is: 'History is made by those who show up.'

18. The Climate Institute, 2013, *Climate of the Nation 2013: Australian Attitudes on Climate Change*, Sydney.

19. Crosby Textor, *Same-Sex Marriage Research 2014: Summary Results*, Sydney, 2014.

20. Gabi Rosenstreich, 2013, *LGBTI People – Mental Health and Suicide*, National LGBTI Health Alliance Briefing Paper, Sydney.

21. Angela Daly. 'Expert Panel: Metadata Retention Report', *The Conversation*, 27 February 2015.

22. New South Wales Council for Civil Liberties. *Metadata Laws: Fighting Crime or Invading Privacy?* media statement, 20 February 2015.

23. Lowy Institute, 2015, *The 2015 Lowy Institute Poll*, Melbourne, p. 6.

CHAPTER 6. SO NOW WHAT?

1. National Centre for Vocational Education Research, 2015, *Australian Vocational Education and Training Statistics: Apprentices and Trainees*, Adelaide.

2. Alice Bednarz, 2014, *Understanding the Non-completion of Apprentices*, National Vocational Education and Training Research Program Occasional Paper, Adelaide; Department of Education, 2014, *Completion Rates of Domestic Bachelor Students – A Cohort Analysis 2005–2013*, Canberra.

3. Hilary Steedman, 2011, *The State of Apprenticeship in 2010*, London School of Economics and Political Science Centre for Economic Performance Working Paper, London.

4. Gavan Conlon et al., 2013, *An International Comparison of Apprentice Pay*, London Economics Working Paper, London.

5. Hilary Steedman, 2011 (see note 3, this chapter).

6. United Voice, *Breakthrough for Cleaners as First Contractors Re-sign Historic Clean Start Collective Agreement*, media statement, 3 December 2013.

7. United Voice, *Big Win for Big Steps Campaign*, media statement, 21 March 2013.

8. United Voice, *Response to Grill'd Founder Simon Crowe's Announcement That He Will 'Modernise' Pay and Conditions of His Workforce*, media statement, 23 July 2015.

9. Chiara Criscuolo, Peter N. Gal and Carlo Menon, 2014, 'The Dynamics of Employment Growth: New Evidence From 18 Countries', *OECD Science Technology and Industry Policy Papers*, Paris.

10. Edmund Tadros and Tim Dodd, 'AFR Top 100 Graduate Employers List: Where Graduates Really Want to Work', *Australian Financial Review*, 16 February 2015.

11. The University of Melbourne, 2014, *Families, Incomes and Jobs. A Statistical Report on Waves 1 to 11 of the Household, Income and Labour Dynamics in Australia Survey*, Melbourne, p. 41.

12. As quoted in Latika Bourke and Judith Ireland, 'Rising House Prices "Causing Social Harm" as Property Bubble Debate Continues', *Sydney Morning Herald*, 7 June 2015.

13. Richard Holden, 2015, *Switching Gears: Reforming Negative Gearing to Solve Our Housing Affordability Crisis*, McKell Institute policy paper, Sydney.

14. Saul Eslake, 2013 (see note 11, chapter 4).

15. John Daley and Danielle Wood, 'Negative Gearing: The Economic Reasons Why Government Must Kill This Sacred Cow', *Sydney Morning Herald*, 17 March 2015.

16. Callam Pickering, 'Why Negative Gearing is Australia's Biggest Policy Failure', *Business Spectator*, 9 July 2014.

17. Index funds let you buy a bundle of stocks in the spread of companies which make up different 'indexes' – such as the All Ordinaries or the ASX 200. Instead of using an investment manager to pick shares – with the attendant risks of getting it wrong and losing big time – the fund invests in whichever companies make up the chosen index. They charge lower fees than managed funds because they don't employ expensive brokers to pick companies for investment. What's more, because they track the market indexes, investors are guaranteed the market return. International and local studies have shown that, on average, index funds tend to perform better than many actively managed funds. That's because while the potential for big returns is reduced, so too is the risk of spectacular losses.

18. Australian Bureau of Statistics. *4221.0 Schools, Australia 2014*. Table 31a Number of schools by affiliation, states and territories. Canberra, 2014; Australian Securities and Investments Commission. *Financial Literacy Program Report 2013–14*. Canberra, 2014

19. Calculations based on 2015 Australian median full-time weekly salary of $1477, at a 5 per cent annual rate of compound interest.

20. Detailed in Joanna Mather, 'Support for a 12.5 Per Cent GST if Stamp Duty Abolished', *Australian Financial Review*, 13 July 2015.

21. Australian Government, 2010, *Super System Review: Final Report*, Canberra, p. 9.

22. Kate Shaw, 'Renting for Life? Housing Shift Requires Rethink Of Renters' Rights', *The Conversation*, 7 January 2014.

23. Feargus O'Sullivan, 'Berlin's New Rent Control Laws Are Already Working', *CityLab*, 9 July 2015.

24. Feargus O'Sullivan, 'Has Germany Figured Out the Way to Keep Rents Affordable?', *CityLab*, 20 November 2013.

25. David W. Nickerson, 2008, 'Is Voting Contagious? Evidence From Two Field Experiments', *American Political Science Review*, Vol. 102, No. 1, pp. 49–57.

26. Thomas Fujiwara, Kyle Meng and Tom Vogl, 2014, 'Estimating Habit Formation in Voting', *MIT Economics Seminar Paper*; Alan S. Gerber, Donald P. Green and Ron Shachar, 2003, 'Voting May Be Habit Forming: Evidence From a Randomized Field Experiment', *American Journal of Political Science*, Vol. 47, No.3, pp. 540–555.

27. Australian Bureau of Statistics, 2013, *3222.0 Population Projections, Australia*, Canberra.

CONCLUSION

1. Martin Parkinson, *University of Adelaide Graduation Address*, speech, University of Adelaide, 6 May 2015.

BATTLERS & BILLIONAIRES
THE STORY OF INEQUALITY IN AUSTRALIA
Andrew Leigh

REDBACK 1

WHY WE ARGUE ABOUT CLIMATE CHANGE
Eric Knight

REDBACK

'Required reading for every Australian who seriously cares about the fair go enduring.' —Peter FitzSimons

'Eric Knight is provoking us to consider not just what we think, but how we think.' —Waleed Aly

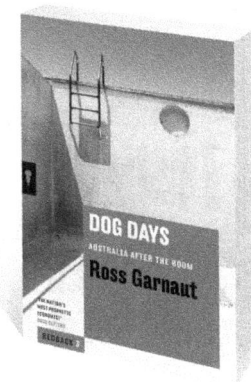

DOG DAYS
AUSTRALIA AFTER THE BOOM
Ross Garnaut

REDBACK 2

ANZAC'S LONG SHADOW
THE COST OF OUR NATIONAL OBSESSION
James Brown

REDBACK 4

'This book is a must-read for anyone concerned with the economic and social future of Australia … lucid, compelling and unburdened by political bias.' —Bob Hawke

'The best book yet written, not just on Australia's Afghan war, but on war itself and the creator/destroyer myth of Anzac.' —John Birmingham

REDBACK QUARTERLY BOOKS WITH BITE

'A reflective, well-argued book ...
Marks also offers suggestions
on a different (better) system of
crime and punishment.'
— *The Sydney Morning Herald*

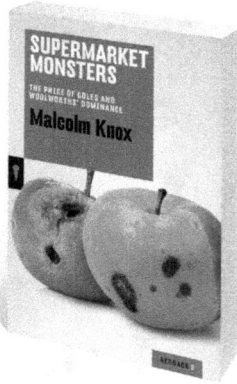

'A valuable primer on the
hidden costs of our
supermarket duopoly.'
— *The Age*

'A brave and personal book, an
anguished account of what
"economic reforms" mean on
the ground.' — *The Australian*

'The best guide you'll find to
the literal non-sense that
usually passes for economic
debate in this country.'
— Ross Gittins

SUBSCRIBE TO REDBACK QUARTERLY
AND SAVE UP TO 25% ON THE COVER PRICE

Enjoy free home delivery of the print edition and full digital access on the
Redback Quarterly website, iPad, iPhone and Android apps.

**FORTHCOMING ISSUES
OF REDBACK QUARTERLY**

**JULY 2016
GUY RUNDLE
ON AUSTRALIA
AND AMERICA**

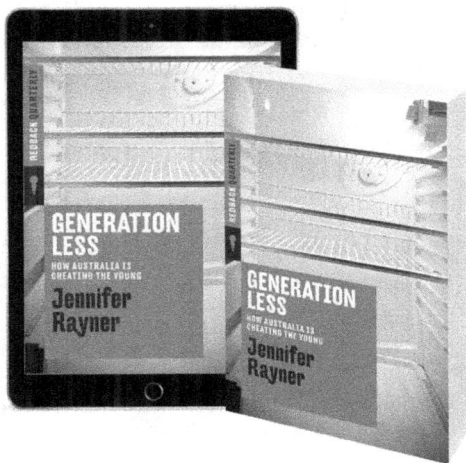

SUBSCRIPTIONS All prices include GST, postage and handling.
Receive a discount and never miss an issue. Mailed direct to your door.

☐ 1 year print and digital subscription (4 issues): $79.95 within Australia.
Outside Australia $119.95.

☐ 1 year print and digital gift subscription (4 issues): $79.95 within Australia.
Outside Australia $119.95.

☐ 2 year print and digital subscription (8 issues): $129.95 within Australia.

☐ 2 year print and digital gift subscription (8 issues): $129.95 within Australia.

☐ 1 year digital only subscription (4 issues): $39.95.

☐ 1 year digital only gift subscription (4 issues): $39.95.

Please turn over for subscription order form, or subscribe online at
REDBACKQUARTERLY.COM.AU
Alternatively, call 1800 077 514 or 03 9486 0288, fax 03 9011 6106
or email subscribe@blackincbooks.com

REDBACK QUARTERLY BACK ISSUES

Prices include GST, postage and handling.

☐ **REDBACK QUARTERLY 1** ($19.99)
*Battlers & Billionaires: The Story
of Inequality in Australia*
by Andrew Leigh

☐ **REDBACK QUARTERLY 3** ($19.99)
Dog Days: Australia After the Boom
by Ross Garnaut

☐ **REDBACK QUARTERLY 4** ($19.99)
*Anzac's Long Shadow: The Cost
of Our National Obsession*
by James Brown

☐ **REDBACK QUARTERLY 5** ($19.99)
*Crime & Punishment: Offenders and
Victims in a Broken Justice System*
by Russell Marks

☐ **REDBACK QUARTERLY 6** ($19.99)
*Supermarket Monsters: The Price of
Coles and Woolworths' Dominance*
by Malcolm Knox

☐ **REDBACK QUARTERLY 7** ($19.99)
*An Economy Is Not a Society:
Winners and Losers in the New
Australia* by Dennis Glover

☐ **REDBACK QUARTERLY 8** ($19.99)
*Econobabble: How to Decode
Political Spin and Economic
Nonsense* by Richard Denniss

Payment Details. I enclose a cheque/money order made out to Schwartz
Publishing Pty Ltd. Please debit my credit card (Mastercard or Visa accepted).

CARD NO. ☐☐☐☐ ☐☐☐☐ ☐☐☐☐ ☐☐☐☐ ☐☐☐☐

EXPIRY DATE   /   **CCV**   **AMOUNT $**

CARDHOLDER'S NAME

NAME

ADDRESS

EMAIL

PHONE

RECIPIENT'S NAME

RECIPIENT'S ADDRESS

Post or fax this form to: Redback Quarterly, Reply Paid 90094, Carlton VIC 3053
Freecall: 1800 077 514 • Tel: (03) 9486 0288 • Fax: (03) 9011 6106
Email: subscribe@blackincbooks.com • Subscribe online at **REDBACKQUARTERLY.COM.AU**

www.ingramcontent.com/pod-product-compliance
Lightning Source LLC
Chambersburg PA
CBHW050651270326
41927CB00012B/2975